DRAMA
Queens

WILD WOMEN OF THE
SILVER SCREEN

AUTUMN STEPHENS

CONARI PRESS
Berkeley, California

Conari Press books are distributed by Publishers Group West.

The photos herein are reprinted by permission of Archive Photo.

Cover Photos: Courtesy of Archive Photo
Handtinting of cover photos: Peggy Lindt
Cover art direction: Ame Beanland
Cover and interior design: Suzanne Albertson

ISBN: 1-57324-136-9

Library of Congress Cataloging-in-Publication Data
Stephens, Autumn.
Drama queens : wild women of the silver screen / Autumn Stephens.
p.   cm.
Includes bibiographical references and index.
ISBN: 1-57324-136-9
1. Motion picture actors and actresses—United States—Biography.
2. Motion picture actors and actresses—United States—Quotations.
3. Actresses—United States—Biography.
4. Actresses—United States—Quotations.   I. Titles.
PN1998.2.S72   1998
791.43'028'0820973—dc21
[b]   98–7867
CIP

Printed in the United States of America on recycled paper
1 3 5 7 9 10 8 6 4 2

To Keasley

To Set the Scene...

*H*ollywood. "A place of mad night life, riotous living, orgies, careers that shot up like meteors and crashed down like lead, uncontrolled extravagances, unbridled love affairs and—in a word—SIN," silent film star Louise Brooks once wrote. SIN, of course, was what that scandalous sex goddess lived for, and the Tinseltown she described was *her* kind of town... until (oops!) the Paramount powers-that-be tried to clue her in to the concept of the work ethic.

Like Brooks, myriad other feminine free spirits have flocked to our famous film capital over the years. Some, of course, have been lured by the decadent attractions of a realm where playing make-believe is a way of life, and fantasy objects are notoriously free to pursue their *own* fantasies. (The kind, needless to say, that would never play in Peoria.) Others have coolly assessed the career options available to persons without penises, and concluded that their faces—or other flawless body parts—really *are* their fortunes.

Then, too, before the rise of the infamously sexist studio system in the mid-1920s, few other venues offered the tremendous opportunities available to women writers, directors, producers, and other professionals who starred *behind* the camera. (Believe it or not, women ruled the movie-making industry prior to 1920—not only did they outnumber men, but their work was considered superior.)

From erotic icons to ball-busting deal-makers, from self-made vamps to congenital tramps, from gnarly non-conformists to flaming crusaders, some of this century's most outrageous scene-makers have called Hollywood home. Here are their sexy, shocking, inspiring—and, yes, deliciously SIN-ful stories.

1

Grande-Standing Dames

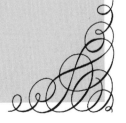

Maverick Mae

No, salacious show biz legend Mae West didn't write the book on sex—though, as we all know, she certainly performed plenty of research in the field. ("Baby, I went to night school," she responded when an interviewer asked how she knew so much about men.) *Sex* was not only the topic, however, but the title of the 1926 stageplay penned by the up-and-coming screen queen that famously landed her in jail on obscenity charges. But it would have taken more than a ten-day stint in the slammer (where, you may recall, West waged a highly publicized battle to wear her own silk underwear) to suppress the bawdy wit of this vampy, campy wisecracker.

"I'm not a little girl from a little town makin' good in a big town," explained the naughty star of the New York stage when she hit Hollywood in 1932. "I'm a big girl from a big town makin' good in a little town." Blonde, blowsy, and so buoyantly buxom that sailors named their inflatable life preservers after her, West was big in more ways than one. The hyper-lascivious leading lady of ten now-classic comedies of the '30s and '40s, she wrote her own lines, collaborated on her own scripts, gave Cary Grant one of his first big breaks by casting him in *I'm No Angel* ("If he can talk, I'll take him," she purred), and single-handedly rescued Paramount from bankruptcy with her starring role in *She Done Him Wrong.* By 1935, West's annual earnings were higher than those of any other woman in America.

Salty rather than sweet, tongue-in-cheek rather than heart-in-hand, sexual aggressor rather than passive love object. . . West toyed with stereotypes about sex and gender like no previous female performer and very few since (with the possible exception of RuPaul). With the on-screen persona of a hotblooded hound dog and the anatomy and complexion of a dairy farmer's daughter, she shattered the femme fatale mold into a thousand tiny

West: The queen of sexy quips

pieces—then glued it back together in a virtually unrecognizable form. "A dame that knows the ropes isn't likely to get tied up," she quipped—and you can bet your bottom dollar that no one tied up Ms. Mae West unless specifically requested to do so.

"When I'm good, I'm very good. But when I'm bad, I'm better."
—MW

THE BEST OF WEST

"Marriage is a great institution, but who wants to be in an institution?"

"The best way to behave is to misbehave."

"Love thy neighbor—and if he happens to be tall, debonair and devastating, it will be that much easier."

"A hard man is good to find."

"When women go wrong, men go right after them."

"Some men are all right in their place—if they only knew the right places!"

"One figure can sometimes add up to a lot."

"It takes two to get one in trouble."

"Give a man a free hand and he tries to put it all over you."

"When caught between two evils, I generally like to take the one I never tried."

"I'm not making a comeback. I never went away!"

THE WORST OF WEST

"[Mae West] is a large, soft, flabby and billowing superblonde who talks through her nostrils and whose laborious ambulations suggest that she has sore feet. She is a menace to art, if not to morals."
—Percy Hammond (movie critic)

"Mae West did have an hourglass figure. She had, besides, a minute attention span."
—Cary Grant

"Mae couldn't sing a lullaby without making it sexy."
—*Variety* Magazine, 1933

"She stole everything but the camera."
—George Raft (as West's co-star in *Night after Night*, ex-lover Raft earned $192/week, i.e., $3,800 less than his former flame)

"She never told the truth in her life."
—Cary Grant

"Is it not time Congress did something about Mae West?"
—William Randolph Hearst

Bad, Bad Bara

"*K*iss me, my fool!" exclaimed silent era star Theda Bara (or so the subtitle on the screen indicated) in her 1915 film debut, *A Fool There Was*. That outrageous line (after all, American women weren't even allowed to vote in 1915, let alone issue explicit amorous requests) helped make the naughty neophyte an overnight sensation. The even more outrageous lines concocted by Bara and her publicists, however, helped keep her in furs and film contracts for four more action-packed years.

By 1919, the then-thirty-something Bara (as loath as any leading lady to reveal her precise date of birth) had made nearly forty movies—and managed to milk her self-made mystique pretty much to death. But what fun the entertainer with the killer eye-liner must have had along the way. Supposedly born in the Sahara to a French artist and his Egyptian mistress, Bara (whose name was an anagram for "Arab Death") played up her pallor, appeared only rarely (and usually heavily veiled) in public, claimed to possess mystical powers, and conducted interviews in dark, incense-filled rooms as she suggestively stroked a snake. Stagey as all this sounds, the public (and even some members of the press) lapped it up like sun-crazed travelers at an oasis.

But if Bara's public persona was a tad over-the-top, so were the dramatic roles she played. Cast as one of the first out-and-out bad girl characters ever to slink across an American screen (hitherto, most parts for actresses might as well have been written for saints), Bara specialized in the role of the ruthless seductress—Carmen, Madame du Barry, Salome, and Cleopatra among them. But her contribution to American culture was not limited to the cinematic arena alone. Fans saw Bara portray a siren who sucked the life (either literally or figuratively) from her man so frequently that they took to

Bara: The epitome of Cincinatti chic

calling her "The Vamp" (short for "The Vampire")—and thus yet another not-always-flattering synonym for "sexy woman" entered the dictionary.

Not that Bara (described by one biographer as "short, bosomy, and a trifle plump") was the type of Nordic-track vixen over whom American moviegoers fawn there days. When it came right down to it, in fact, Bara wasn't even *Bara*. Though her most devoted fans chose to overlook the fact, many were aware that she was born plain old Theodosia Goodman, the daughter of a Cincinnati (not a Saharan) tailor.

Nonetheless, the Midwesterner in mufti (and a few strategically-placed spangles) was considered pretty hot stuff in her heyday. As the story goes, the presumed hussy and "husband stealer" (in fact, Bara seems to have been a disappointingly faithful wife) once sparked a small riot by admiring a hat in a department store. Immediately throngs of female admirers rushed in to paw at said chapeau, hoping to pick up some of the bespangled one's sultry allure in the process.

Even at the height of her popularity, Bara was not renowned for any out-of-the-ordinary thespian talents. "She is pretty bad, but not enough to be remembered always," opined critic Alexander Wollcott. But obviously Mr. Wollcott wasn't nearly as clairvoyant as the target of his barb sometimes claimed to be. We do remember brazen Bara today—not as a great actress, of course, but as an American original who had the moxie (and the publicists) to just make it up as she went along.

"It's all just make-believe."
—TB

Hairy Mary

When sixteen-year-old Mary Pickford made her screen debut in 1909, audiences could identify her only as "Little Mary," or the "Girl with the Golden Hair." Not without reason (ahem!), early producers feared that actors might develop swollen heads and bloated salary expectations if their names were listed in a picture's credits.

A few years down the road, however, few Americans didn't know the given name of pixieish Pickford, the biggest box-office draw of her day, and the country's first bona fide movie star. Cast primarily in demure, sweet-to-saccharine parts, the "Girl with the Golden Hair" so captivated a nation unaccustomed to the novelty of the cinema that she was soon promoted to the position of "America's Sweetheart."

In contrast to her naive screen image, however, the teen sensation proved a shrewd businesswoman. The family breadwinner, due to the death of her father, from an early age, Pickford finessed D. W. Griffith into giving her a raise the same day she was hired. And that was just the beginning: strategically hopping from studio to studio, Pickford negotiated increasingly higher salaries as she went, reaching the then-astounding of sum of $350,000 a picture in 1917—plus a share of the box office. "She talks money, discusses contracts and makes important decisions with disconcerting speed," marvelled director Ernst Lubitsch, yet "nothing of this prevents her from playing scenes filled with sweetness and passion."

Not surprisingly, Pickford's tenacity at the bargaining table sometimes set teeth on edge. "She had the nerve to tell me she couldn't afford to work for a mere $10,000 a week," huffed Paramount's Adolph Zukor, while Samuel Goldwyn complained that "it took longer to make one of Mary's contracts than it did to make one of Mary's pictures."

Yet loot wasn't always the bottom line for the dimpled charmer: Pickford demanded the final say in decisions regarding scripts (not coincidentally, her pal Frances Marion wrote most of her films), casting, directors, and advertising. According to some accounts, she even directed most of her own movies, but claimed no credit in order to preserve her maidenly image. And in 1919, the "Girl with the Golden Hair" famously joined forces with Griffith, Charlie Chaplin, and Douglas Fairbanks to create United Artists Corporation, the first company ever formed to distribute the films of independent producers.

Pickford's private affairs, however, defied her chronic desire for iron-clad control. Spouse number one, actor Owen Moore, wound up an incorrigible (and divorced) alcoholic. Millions were thrilled by Pickford's second marriage, to screen idol/business partner Fairbanks, and sighed over tales of the couple's fairy-tale love affair. But Cupid soon fled from Pickfair, the magnificent mansion named equally after husband and wife, and eventually Pickford wound up in divorce court again.

Strange but true: with bound breasts and still-cascading curls, Pickford starred in *Pollyanna* at the age of twenty-seven, and in *Little Lord Fauntleroy*—as both mother *and* son—the following year. If her fans had had their way, in fact, she would still have been playing juvenile parts when she died. Judging from the public outcry when she finally sheared her childish mane, the then-thirty-six-year-old Pickford observed, "you would think I had murdered someone." "And," she added astutely, "in a sense, I had." Though Pickford won an Academy Award for her chicly-bobbed performance in *Coquette* (her first talkie) in 1929, audiences simply refused to accept the girl *without* her golden hair, and she retired from the screen in 1933.

The recipient of a special Oscar recognizing her contribution to American film in 1975, Pickford (whose post-Hollywood occupations included publishing several books and founding a cosmetics company) died four years later. As for her other great contribution to American culture—well, snippets of the star's trademark tresses are always on display, should you care to see them, at various Los Angeles and San Diego museums.

> *"Say anything you like about me, but don't say I 'like' to work.*
> *That sounds like Mary Pickford, that prissy bitch."*
> —Mabel Normand, Pickford's
> pleasure-loving contemporary

Appalling Pola

Pola Negri was born in 1899 to a Polish noblewoman and a Slovakian revolutionary—unless, that is, she was born in 1894, or 1897, or her mother was an impoverished nobody, or her father was a Gypsy violinist, or…well, you get the general dubious drift. One thing we know for sure, however, is that Negri (née Barbara Apolonia Chalupiec) had a very artistic temperament, and the hell with the technical details of her origins, which she (and later, studio spin doctors) embellished as she pleased.

The tempestuous star of several significant German films, Negri was snapped up by Paramount in 1923 as their answer to MGM's European import, Greta Garbo. Well, Negri was no Queen Christina (although she *did* portray Catherine the Great in the 1924 film *Forbidden Paradise*), and the statuesque Swede wasn't exactly toppled from her throne. Unlike understated Garbo, however, Negri had quite a knack for histrionics, and she enthralled American audiences as the exotic, erotic, unabashedly neurotic leading lady of several financially-successful pictures.

So popular was the impassioned Pole in her day, in fact, that her influence extended from the box office to the cosmetics counter and back. Following in the still-smoldering footsteps of Cincinnati vamp Theda Bara, Negri revived the fad for chalk-white face powder and kohl, and hitherto healthy fashionplates suddenly took on a Halloweenish pallor. (Trendy '20s gals, however, accessorized the perennially-sexy death's door look with ropes of pearls instead of Doc Martens.) Frankly, however, some found the screen queen's sense of style a little frightening. "Her toes are bleeding!" screamed one fan, who, like most Americans at the time, had never seen a woman wearing toenail polish.

Negri also exerted quite a powerful (not to mention P.R.-enhancing) pull on her

Pola and pal bask in the limelight

fellow stars. Charlie Chaplin, for one, came down with a case of Pola-io so severe that, at Negri's direction, he called a press conference to announce his matrimonial intentions. Rudolph Valentino, too, suffered from the malady for a time—supposedly the love-sick sheik declared *his* intentions by scattering rose petals on her bed. As for Negri—well, her feelings for Rudy were so deep (and her sense of a good photo op so unerring) that she dolled herself up in a $3,000 mourning ensemble for his funeral and proceeded to faint, frequently and flamboyantly, for the cameras. Between swoons, the Bereaved Beauty recovered enough to drop another image-enhancing bomb: she and The Great Lover, she claimed, had been betrothed at the time of his premature death.

This revelation came as quite a shock to Ziegfeld star Marion Brenda (among many, many others), who seemed to recall that Valentino had begged for *her* hand just hours before he was felled by fatal peritonitis. Tallulah Bankhead, too, remained singularly unmoved by Negri's post-mortem confession. "The biggest phony in Hollywood!" she scoffed. "A lying lesbo, a Polish publicity hound!" And for good measure, she added that Negri "couldn't act her way out of a paper bag."

Naturally, Valentino's putative valentine did not share Bankhead's assessment of her talents. "I consider my work great and I am a great actress," she informed one admirer who had mistakenly described her as merely "charming." But by the late '20s, American moviegoers had begun to find Negri's over-the-top shtick more dated than daring, and she returned to Germany, where she continued her career with renewed success. A tiny snafu once arose when Nazi officials concluded that Negri was a Jew (as *if* anyone ever got a good peek at her rather fluid family tree), and propaganda minister Joseph Goebbels tried to ban her from the screen. But no dice: Hitler himself vetoed his henchman's command, being so fond of Negri's 1935 tearjerker *Mazurka* that he viewed it on a weekly basis.

A recluse in the final decades of her long and dramatic life, Negri died in San Antonio in 1987 at the advanced age of...well, who knows. Long before shuffling (or slinking, more likely) off this mortal coil, however, the mistress of mystique-mongering set the world straight on at least one of the particulars of her past. Contrary to the rumors, she asserted, the Fuhrer had never been her bedmate, and she successfully sued the pants off the French movie magazine *Pour Vous* for alleging otherwise. Even for the notoriously opportunistic Pola Negri, it seems, that particular publicity opportunity just wasn't worth cashing in on.

"I was European, and therefore, I was temperamental."
—PN

Sister Act

Though silent screen stars Lillian and Dorothy Gish shared the same line of work—and sometimes the same film set as well— sibling rivalry just wasn't part of the picture. No tawdry tooth-and-nail catfights, à la savage sisters Joan Fontaine and Olivia de Havilland, for these two class acts. In fact, the Gish girls were so close that it was sometimes whispered that they were secret lovers.

Born in 1896 and 1898, respectively, little Lillian and Dorothy were barely out of diapers when they started proving that sisterhood was powerful (and darn cute on stage, as well). By the time they were pre-schoolers, their combined income from acting in stage melodramas was keeping mother Mary (a struggling single mom) out of the poorhouse.

In 1912, the Gish-ettes got a mondo break when they ran into Gladys Smith, a long-lost childhood friend—who was now, it turned out, Mary Pickford, the most famous film star in America. Pickford put in a good word for them with director D.W. Griffith, and that same day, Lillian and Dorothy began acting in their first film, Griffith's *An Unseen Enemy*. (Good old Mom got a bit part, too.) To top off this fabulous fairy tale, sixteen-year-old Lillian turned out to be the princess of D.W.'s dreams (professionally speaking, anyway), and his favorite leading lady for years to come. "She is not only the best actress in her profession," he would later gush, "but she has the best mind of any woman I have ever met."

Griffith wasn't alone in his awe of Lillian's talents. Her roles in classics of the '20s like *Orphans of the Storm* and *The Scarlet Letter* earned her numerous over-the-top nicknames ("Lillian the Incomparable" and "The World's Darling" among them). They also almost earned her a premature plot in the cemetery. Though she tried to toughen up for her blizzard scenes in the 1920 melodrama *Way Down East* by taking ice-baths, her face nonetheless froze during shooting. And to transform herself into a convincingly consumptive Mimi in

La Bohème, she pared so many pounds from her already petite-frame that director King Vidor feared she would perish as tragically as her character.

Dramatic in every sense of the word, Lillian's career may simply have kept her too busy to bother with a spouse. Or perhaps, as many have suggested, she never married because she preferred women. "Oh, dear," she supposedly sighed as she arrived on the *La Bohème* set in 1926. "I've got to go through another day of kissing John Gilbert."

Unlike Lillian, the putative lipstick lesbian, Dorothy never had the benefit of being Griffith's pet protégé. Frankly, the director didn't think much of the younger Miss Gish's perky acting style. But when Lillian strong-armed Griffith into casting Dorothy as a comic minstrel in *Hearts of the World* in 1918, Little Sister stole the show, and wound up with a million-dollar, two-year contract offer from Paramount-Artcraft Studios. Only twenty years old at the time, she also wound up as the first (and probably the last) actress ever to turn down such a lucrative offer because "at my age all that money would ruin my character."

Eventually, unspoiled, unwealthy Dorothy blossomed into one of the most popular and prolific comic actresses of her era, sometimes compared to Charlie Chaplin and Buster Keaton. But while audiences ate up ethereal Lillian's damsel-in-distress dramas, Dorothy groused that fewer people wanted "to see a woman play outright comedy" (a complaint still voiced by comediennes today).

Fortunately, however, Dorothy didn't feel too funny about the delicious Gishes' differing genres to team up with her sister for *Remodeling Her Husband* in 1920. Lillian directed, Dorothy starred as a new bride, James Rennie played the groom, and before the end of the year, the celluloid husband wound up as Dorothy's flesh-and-blood spouse—and, of course, Lillian's brother-in-law. And that, my dears, is a *genuinely* incestuous situation for you.

"We weren't doing it for the money."

—LG

Battle-Ax Bette

One of the most-hated divas in Hollywood, Bette Davis certainly didn't wind up as "the first lady of the American screen" by making nice. Tenacious, temperamental, and unafraid to pick a fight, Davis was the type who clawed her way to the top—and the hell with the old honey-versus-vinegar theory of fly entrapment.

The Abraham Lincoln of the silver screen, so to speak, Davis was no great beauty, and apparently no great shakes as an actress, either, in her younger days. Rejected by a prestigious drama school, fired from a summer stock production, and laughed out of town after one abysmal screen test, the twenty-two-year-old actress finally landed a Universal contract in 1930...only to be told she was "not sexy enough" to play the role for which she had supposedly been brought on board.

Bloody but unbowed, Davis went on to make several films at Warner Brothers before she finally engineered her own big break in 1934, demanding that the studio release her to play loathsome Mildred Rogers in *Of Human Bondage* at RKO. Unlike Davis, none of RKO's actresses cared to be cast as a spiteful bitch, but Davis won an Academy Award nomination for screaming things like "You cad! You dirty swine!" in an impassioned landmark performance.

And speaking of bitch...that's precisely what the newly-minted Ms. Thing proceeded to do back at Warner Brothers. Grousing about "inferior roles" and "slavelike working conditions," pushing for more vacations and loan-outs—as time went on, Davis got to be one very squeaky wheel. Needless to say, the constant kvetch-fest made Warners grumpy, and they got even grumpier when the actress flat-out refused to make *Satan Meets a Lady* for them.

BETTE BITES BACK

"It's only the best fruit the birds pick at."

"I do not regret one professional enemy I have made. Any actor who doesn't dare to make an enemy should get out of the business."

"I am just too much."

"I was thought to be 'stuck up.' I wasn't. I was just sure of myself. This is and always has been an unforgivable quality to the unsure."

"I am a queen."

"I know I've been a perfect bitch. But I couldn't help myself."

Blowout battles, Davis' first suspension, and her stormy, contract-violating exodus to make two films in England followed. To top it all off, Warners even sued Davis for breach of contract, and won a judgment against her. But check it out: once the sparks stopped flying, the studio treated Davis with greater respect, and finally started feeding her plum parts. The squeaky wheel, in short, had encountered the grease.

Marked Woman, Jezebel, Dark Victory, The Little Foxes, The Corn Is Green, All About Eve, What Ever Happened To Baby Jane?, Hush Hush Sweet Charlotte, The Whales of August ... from the mid-1930s through the late 1980s, Davis compiled the resume on which her status as one of the greatest movie stars of all time rests. Still, the camera didn't capture *all* of her dramatic performances: unmellowed by time or acclaim, the maverick actress waged war on directors, feuded with co-stars, and railed about the inferior quality of American manhood.

(Not one of her four spouses, she once complained, "was man enough to become Mr. Bette Davis.") On what must have been slow days, gripe-wise, she even bickered with the Academy of Motion Picture Arts and Sciences about the origin of the term "Oscar."

Nominated for ten Academy Awards during the course of her career, Davis pocketed two (for *Dangerous* in 1935 and *Jezebel* in 1938), as well as the New York Film Critics award for *All About Eve* in 1950, and the first American Film Institute's Life Achievement Award ever given to a woman. All the more impressive, when you consider that few of her triumphs would have been possible without the use of her talons. To a dog-eat-dog philosopher like Davis, however, such was simply the way of the world. "Until you're known in my profession as a monster," she once noted, "you're not a star."

> *"You know what they'll write on my tombstone? 'She did it the hard way.'"*
> —BD

The self-described "perfect bitch"

The Meanest Mother in Hollywood

*A*ccording to some, Joan Crawford was never a class act to begin with. "She's slept with every male star at MGM except Lassie," snorted arch-rival Bette Davis (not unfamiliar with the mink-like mode herself). "That terrible, vulgar woman with the pop eyes beats her children," sniffed Marlene Dietrich. "But what do you expect from that class—a cheap tap dancer." And if you really want to get down and dirty—well, we understand that early in her career, Crawford cared so little for personal hygiene that wardrobe assistants picked up her discarded garments with sticks.

A laundress, a waitress, a hat saleswoman, and a Broadway chorus girl before she came to MGM's attention in 1925, Crawford even made a couple of porn films (*Velvet Lips* and *The Casting Couch*) in her flaming youth. (If you have a hard time picturing "Mommie Dearest" in the throes of lesbian passion, check out the stills in Kenneth Anger's second superb scandalography, *Hollywood Babylon II.*) Yet hard work and boundless ambition (and the fact that MGM categorically denied her checkered past) made this wrong-side-of-the-tracks Sally one of Hollywood's most enduring stars.

Termed "the best example of a flapper" by none other than F. Scott Fitzgerald, the definitive Roaring Twenties novelist, Crawford first made a name for herself as a Clara Bow type, most notably in *Our Dancing Daughters* (1928). But that was only the beginning. Depression-era working gals, broad-shouldered women of the world, a long-suffering (and Academy Award-winning) mother in *Mildred Pierce* (1945), even a scream queen in *What Ever Happened To Baby Jane?* (1962) . . . Crawford went on to play them all, in the course of a career that spanned nearly half a century.

Married five times (most notably to Douglas Fairbanks, Jr. and Alfred Steele, the Pepsi-Cola tycoon) and mated with many, many others, Crawford and her erotic escapades provided abundant grist for the Hollywood gossip mill. Asked what sparked her passion for *Possessed* co-star Clark Gable, she responded bluntly: "Balls. He had them." And according to *Hollywood Lesbians* author Boze Hadleigh, Joan was even romantically linked with butch director Dorothy Arzner.

Nor was the former porn actress shy about claiming the various perqs of celebrity-hood. Toasted French bread and seven packages of cigarettes (three of them opened) had to be waiting when she arrived at her hotel room—or else! At any given time, she owned at least two hundred pairs of shoes. More shades of Imelda: in 1932, Crawford published a piece in *Photoplay* asserting her privilege as a movie star—her duty, in fact—to maintain herself in lavish style. (Meanwhile, of course, her fellow Americans were plunging from upper-story windows and living in Hoovervilles.) And to keep her ego stoked on the set, Crawford even hired a gentleman whose sole responsibility to whisper outrageous compliments in her ear. Seems that the technique worked, too: "I like to think that every director I've worked with has fallen a little in love with me," the consummate prima donna once bragged.

Unfortunately, while Crawford was busy polishing her professional image, she failed to devote equal attention to her maternal obligations. Or so daughter Christina famously alleged in her bitter 1978 bestseller, *Mommie Dearest*. Since Crawford had died the previous year, she was unable to respond to charges that she was the cruelest coathanger-wielder to come down the pike since Cinderella's stepmother, or to catch Faye Dunaway's 1981 portrayal of her poor parenting skills. It's a cinch, however, that this grand old lady of the cinema wouldn't have cared much for her post-mortem make-over as, in the words of one film reviewer, "a combination of Medea and Medusa."

"I was as civil as I knew how to be."
—JC

TROUBLESOME TWOSOMES

Two big egos. Two short fuses. One hell of an explosion. And another dynamite entry in the Annals of Feuding Film Stars . . .

Bogie and Bacall had a grand passion. So did Newman and Woodward. And so, we submit, did Bette Davis and Joan Crawford, two temperamental superstars whose mutual obsession ran even deeper than love. "Joan Crawford—Hollywood's first case of syphilis," Davis once spat. "I wouldn't sit on her toilet!" "Take away the pop eyes, the cigarette, and those funny clipped words, and what have you got? She's phony, but I guess the public likes that," hissed Crawford. It's said that the famed feud dated back to 1935, when Davis bedded *Dangerous* co-star Franchot Tone, Crawford's husband at the time. Of course, it's also said that Crawford herself wouldn't have minded doing Davis—or was that doing her in? Ah, the proverbial thin line. . .

One of Hollywood's most ubiquitous sparring partners, Davis also had herself a little dust-up with Miriam Hopkins. Some say it started when Davis spurned an offer to share Hopkins' bed. Some claim that Hopkins turned hostile when Davis took up with her husband. And others, bless their cynical little hearts, blame the whole thing on the Warner Brothers publicity department. Whoever did (or didn't) do what to whom, however, the upshot certainly seems to have been palpable acrimony. "I didn't direct them," explained Vincent Sherman, who encountered the problematic pair on the set of *Old Acquaintance* in 1943. "I refereed."

Talk about catty! When movie star Lupe Velez was peeved at chanteuse Libby Holman, her co-star in a Broadway production of *You Never Know*, she supposedly would urinate on the floor just outside Holman's dressing room.

★ ★ ★

One year in age—and one thousand petty grudges—separated squabbling sibs Olivia de Havilland (born in 1916) and Joan Fontaine (born in 1917). Of course, it didn't help that the rivalrous relatives were both nominated for the Best Actress Academy Award in the same year. "I married first, won the Oscar before Olivia did, and if I die first she'll undoubtedly be livid because I beat her to it," tee-heed Fontaine, the sister who went home with the statue in 1941. "Can you imagine what it's like to be an elder sister and have your younger one do everything first?" pouted de Havilland, who finally snagged her Academy Award in 1946—and another one (so ha ha ha, Joanie!) three years later. One photo, snapped on the occasion of de Havilland's 1946 victory, says it all: ticked-off despite her triumph, the Best Actress in American film conspicuously turns her back on her sister.

★ ★ ★

"What do you expect me to do?" man-trap Elizabeth Taylor once quipped. "Sleep alone?" Well, actually, that was precisely what actress Debbie Reynolds expected of Taylor, a friend of hubby Eddie Fisher and herself. But in 1958, shortly after Taylor was widowed, Reynolds learned that Fisher was doing more than just patting the violet-eyed vixen's hand. In the great tradition of Tammy Wynette and Hillary Clinton, Reynolds stood by her man. "I am still in love with my husband," she insisted. "Do not blame

him for what has happened." (And here we thought it took two to tango.) For what it was worth, the world sided with Reynolds, and her popularity soared. Meanwhile, the happy homewrecker threw a so-called "You Can All Go To Hell" party to celebrate her latest acquisition.

Once upon a time, actress-cum-talk-show-guest Elke Sommer derided the size of Zsa Zsa Gabor's derriere. Gabor retaliated in not-so-kind, terming Sommer a balding barfly, or words to that effect. Sommer, who apparently is not a balding barfly, won a $3.3 million judgment against Gabor for calling her one. But there the matter did not rest. In early 1998, Sommer slapped another libel suit on Gabor's current spouse, who supposedly misspoke when he said that Sommer said that "All German men are pigs." We eagerly await developments.

Great Kate

Feminine wiles were never part of Katharine Hepburn's repertoire. They didn't have to be. A striking, patrician presence in a sea of girl-next-door types and sex goddesses, the twelve-time Academy Award nominee wrote her own ticket both off the screen and on.

Fittingly, it was the twenty-five-year-old actress's stage performance as an Amazon queen in *The Warrior's Husband* that brought her to RKO's attention in 1932. Since Hollywood had little appeal for Hepburn at the time, she jokingly told the studio that she wouldn't sign a contract for less than $1,500 a week—and was stunned when they accepted her then-exorbitant demand. Less than two years later, the diffident movie star won her first Oscar for *Morning Glory. (Guess Who's Coming to Dinner* [1967], *The Lion in Winter* [1968], and *On Golden Pond* [1981] would also net her Academy Awards.)

Labeled "box office poison" by the Independent Theatre Owners Association in the late 1930s (androgynous-looking colleagues Joan Crawford, Greta Garbo, and Marlene Dietrich shared the distinction), Hepburn returned to the stage. Five years later, however, she was back in Hollywood, this time holding a winning hand. During her absence, she had starred in the Broadway production of *The Philadelphia Story,* shrewdly accepting film rights in lieu of a salary. MGM was eager to snap up the option, and a triumphant Hepburn dictated the choice of director and leads (one of whom, of course, was herself). And from then to the end of her fabled career in the 1980s, she succeeded in calling her own shots.

No one ever termed Hepburn a sex symbol, though her prominent cheekbones, columnist Art Buchwald once quipped, constituted "the greatest calcium deposit since the White Cliffs of Dover." Nearly as aloof as Garbo, and even less fond of feminine garb (much to the chagrin of various studios), she scorned reporters, shunned public appearances, and shielded herself behind her WASPish New England wit. "Trying to be fascinating is an asinine position to be in," she once said. Remarkably, reporters respected her wishes. Even her twenty-five-year-long romance with married man Spencer Tracy, her frequent on-screen sparring partner, remained a taboo topic for gossip columnists until after Tracy's death in 1967.

"If you survive, you become a legend," Hepburn once said. "I'm a legend because I've survived over a long period of time." With all due respect to one of Hollywood's most hallowed stars (now in her nineties, and reportedly in failing health), it seems that there's a little more to the Katharine "I Did It My Way" Hepburn story than an exceptionally long run.

"My privacy is my own and I am the one to decide when it shall be violated."

—*KH*

Heretical Hepburn in her heyday

Mammy Cleans Up

When Mae West commanded her maid Beulah to "peel me a grape" in the 1933 film *I'm No Angel*, the line brought down the house. More than sixty years later, however, moviegoers aren't quite so quick to chuckle at that classically demeaning quip. And while Hattie McDaniel, the black actress who played Mae's minion, viewed her role rather pragmatically, she probably didn't find the mistress/slave premise a real barrel of laughs, either. In fact, West's thirty-eight-year-old sidekick knew more than she wanted to about subservience, having sometimes worked as a real-life maid (one of the few forms of employment then available to black women) to make ends meet. And it was déjà vu all over again in the reel world: invariably, the accomplished singer/actress wound up doing the dusting or the dishes.

In 1939, however, McDaniel finally got a shot at the *other* role available to members of her sex and race. Cast, despite concerns about her lack of "dignity" and "nobility," in the coveted role of Mammy in *Gone With the Wind*, she became the first African American woman to win an Academy Award for Best Supporting Actress. (There wouldn't be a second until 1990, when Whoopi Goldberg picked up her Oscar for *Ghost*.) "I sincerely hope that I shall always be a credit to my race," McDaniel said in her acceptance speech, "and to the motion picture industry." The motion picture industry, however, wasn't exactly a credit to *her*—neither she nor any other black actors were allowed to attend the movie's Atlanta premiere, since producer David Selznick felt their presence would make Southern audiences uncomfortable (read: unprofitable).

Like many an actress before and since, McDaniel didn't hesitate to cash in on her triumph: she appeared in public in full "Mammy" regalia, posed for photos with her collection of mammy figurines, and even published recipes for "Mammy's fried chicken."

McDaniel schlepped her way to the top

Lambasted by the NAACP, she responded by co-founding the Fair Play Committee, a black actors' organization that fought film industry racism. But when reformers criticized the former domestic worker for capitalizing on a servile role, she had only one comment: "Hell, I'd rather play a maid than be one!"

"There are only eighteen inches between a pat on the back and a kick in the rump."
—HM

SHOW ME THE MONEY

Back in 1963, Elizabeth Taylor made film (and financial) history when she pulled down the unheard-of sum of $1,000,000 to play the part of Cleopatra. Today, of course, a paltry one million will scarcely get you to the other side of the Nile—let alone a write-up in *Entertainment Weekly*. And in Hollywood as in Hoboken, the male of the species continues to command heftier fees for virtually identical work (except, of course, that the guys aren't asked to doff their garb quite so often). Still, at least a handful of top-grossing screen goddesses aren't having too much trouble making their mortgage payments these days...

GROSS

Geena Davis: $7 million for *Cutthroat Island* (1996)

Whoopi Goldberg: $8 million for *Sister Act II* (1993)

GROSSER

Sandra Bullock: $10.5 million for *In Love and War* (1997)

Sigourney Weaver: $11.25 million for *Alien Resurrection* (1977)

GROSSEST

Julia Roberts: $12 million for *My Best Friend's Wedding* (1997)

Demi Moore: $12.5 million for *Striptease* (1996)

FAMOUS LAST WORDS

Everyone's a critic—and nowhere more so than in Hollywood, where even the world's most talented and tantalizing women don't always live up to a director's (or a co-star's, or a cameraman's) airbrushed fantasies. In fact, if they'd paid any mind to their supposed minuses, some of our favorite screen-stealers would have wound up on the cutting room floor—clutching a hara kiri knife...

"You're too little and too fat," pronounced D.W. Griffith, "but I may give you a chance." The chubby shortstuff in question was none other than sixteen-year-old Mary Pickford, who blossomed into the prolific, popular, and top-grossing silent star known as "America's Sweetheart."

Jutting Jane Russell was deemed "too tall" (by Paramount) and too "unphotogenic" (by Twentieth Century-Fox) to make it big, as it were, in pictures.

Okay, so maybe it wasn't a huge stretch for Louise "Your Bed or Mine?" Brooks to play a naughty nymphomaniac in the 1926 classic, *Pandora's Box*. But actor Richard Arlen certainly called it wrong when he told the legend-to-be, "You're a lousy actress and your eyes are too close together."

"She is quite impossible to photograph: too tall, too big-boned, too heavy all around," complained the first cameraman to try to capture voluptuous Sophia Loren on film. "What do you want of me, miracles?"

Samuel Goldwyn was not impressed with young actress's first screen test. "Who did this to me?" he bellowed. Well, actually, Bette Davis did.

According to Susan Myrick, the dialect expert for *Gone with the Wind*, Hattie McDaniel just didn't make a credible "Mammy." "She lacks dignity, age, nobility... and she hasn't the right face for it." McDaniel won an Oscar for her performance in the film.

Not yet ubiquitous singer/actress/*Sex* author Madonna behaved so badly at a MTV Video Music Awards rehearsal in 1984 that one attendee confidently predicted, "Her career is over before it started."

Louis B. Mayer initially took a pass on Swedish sphinx Greta Garbo. "We don't like fat girls in my country," he announced. All-American Ava Gardner, however, scored higher on the Mayer meter. "She can't act. She can't talk. She's terrific," he ambivalated. (Of course, Ava wasn't a heifer...)

"…Her bottom droops a bit, and you can discern incipient cellulite on her thighs," wrote the movie critic, describing the lovely actress's role in the surreal and controversial *Blue Velvet*. This incisive critique of her talents notwithstanding, former Lancôme model Isabella Rossellini is still widely believed to be one of the most beautiful women in the world.

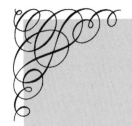

2

Sexcess Goddesses

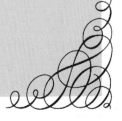

Bow Wow

Clara Bow, the flame-haired "It" girl of the Roaring '20s, had a Brooklyn accent, a brash, unrefined manner, and a mentally-ill mother who, she claimed, once tried to stab her with a butcher knife to prevent her from becoming a "Hollywood whore." But Bow, who was sixteen when she landed her first film role (as the prize for winning a movie magazine beauty contest) was luckier—and pluckier—than most. The accent would remain irrelevant until "the talkies" came along a few years later, with-it girls of the Jazz Age weren't *supposed* to be ladies, and not even Mom's stab at career counseling could keep Bow from chasing her dream (though it did cause her lifelong insomnia).

Sensual, Cupid-bow lips and a shrink-wrapped approach to her attire undoubtedly helped Bow get a foothold in the film industry. Hard work, however, kept her there—by the end of her first year in Hollywood, she had already appeared in more than a dozen films, and was considered a star in the making. Almost invariably cast as a flapper (complete with cropped coiffure, short skirts, and a devil-may-care attitude toward most of the standard vices), Bow eventually grew to loathe portraying the type. Yet her vibrant turn as yet another card-carrying member of the bobbed-hair set in the 1927 film *It* catapulted her to the top of the Hollywood heap. Two years later, Bow—an eighth-grade drop-out from the slums—had become the highest-paid actress in the industry.

Bow was a very busy girl off-screen, as well. "Clara Bow laid everything except the linoleum," the joke went, and a wicked rumor circulated that she especially enjoyed "entertaining" the entire University of Southern California football team. Not that the so-called "Mountie of Sex" (yes, Bow always got her man) didn't have her share of serious suitors—she just had them several at a time. "Clara's engagements are about as

Clara contemplates her conquests

frequent and enduring as the average girl's headaches," snickered one columnist.

But Bow would brook no criticism of her social habits. When fiance Harry Richman got huffy over her fling with Gary Cooper, she explained that monogamy just wasn't part of her game plan—take it, or leave it. Nor did she cave when Hollywood's moral watchdog, The Hays Office, complained that the "It" girl was doing more than just *symbolizing* sex (apparently she had been seen in public once too often with a married lover). Marry Harry, she was told, or get out of Hollywood for good. Bow did neither—and *The Wedding Night*, her next picture, was a raging success.

A torrent of scandals (financial as well as sexual), however, forever tarnished the luster of Paramount's former sweetheart in the early 1930s. A Hollywood has-been in her mid-twenties, Bow married B-movie cowboy Rex Bell, did a stint or two in a mental hospital, and simply refused to write her memoirs, lest her children find the truth about Mom's time in Tinseltown too shocking. "I don't want to be remembered," she once explained, "as somebody who couldn't do anything but take her clothes off."

> *"Being a sex symbol is a heavy load to carry."*
> —CB

FULL OF "IT"

A red-hot siren with scarlet hair and a reputation to match, Clara Bow rose to fame (and plunged to notoriety) as the "It" Girl of the Jazz Age. But what, precisely, *was* "It?"

According to historian Lois Banner, "It" all started with English romance novelist and screenwriter Elinor Glyn, who used the word as an "idiosyncratic euphemism for sex appeal." Ms. Glyn's vocabulary became somewhat less idiosyncratic, however, when Paramount publicists learned that the wildly popular author had singled out Bow as the epitome of "It." Faster than you could snap a flapper's garter, Bow was catapulting her way to etymological immortality in Paramount's 1927 film *It*, which was based on Glyn's sexy novelette titled—yes, you guessed it—*It*.

Womens' biographer Jennifer Uglow also finds "It" a near synonym for "Id." In her egalitarian book, however, "It"-ness wasn't the exclusive personal property of Bow: the prominent (and prominently promiscuous) star merely symbolized the "It" inherent in all "American women of the 1920s who smoked, drank, wore daring clothes and were sexually brave."

Cinema chronicler Ephraim Katz, on the other hand, manages to make "It" sound like an especially perky, fresh-faced member of the pep squad. (Bow was, of course, rumored to be fond of the members of a certain athletic team, but that's a different story, and one that the gentlemanly and probably lawsuit-free Mr. Katz left for less discreet souls to tell.) According to Katz, "It" merely meant "the unself-conscious attraction of the modern young woman—that 'something extra' that separated her from the ordinary crowd."

As far as _we're_ concerned, however, it was no less an authority than actress Susan Hayward (like Bow, a star with hair of a dramatic hue) who really put her finger squarely on the thrumming, erotically-charged pulse of "It." No wonder "Clara Bow had 'It,'" Hayward concluded. "She caught 'It' from receiving too many passes from too many football players."

Platinum Power

*N*o career counselor in her right mind would advise you to wear a black crocheted dress—let alone nada, nada, nada underneath—your first day on a new job. Precisely such a peekaboo number, however, was what eighteen-year-old Jean Harlow was sporting when she slithered onto the set of *Saturday Night Kid* in 1929. Leading lady Clara Bow promptly tried to fire the knockout newcomer, assistant director Artie Johnson became fascinated by the fact that Harlow appeared to be a natural (or at least a consistent) blonde, and yet another "reigning sex goddess" (as gossip columnists would soon be calling her) of Hollywood was born.

At her best in "bad girl" roles, Harlow lifted the spirits (among other things) of a Depressed nation with her suggestive smile, rapidfire retorts, and subtle comedic flair in '30s classics like *Red Dust* and *Hell's Angels*. A habit of icing her nipples before filming a scene didn't hurt her career any, either. And off-screen, too, "The Platinum Blonde" (a nickname taken from her 1931 film of that title) exuded sensuality—a fact that her publicists played up to the hilt. Harlow, it was widely known, was as fond of mink as the next movie star—and probably the only Hollywood hedonist who regularly went to work wearing pelts over her PJs. The word was that she also enjoyed the feel of fur against her skin, eschewed lingerie because it inhibited her breathing, and slept in the nude—in a bed modeled on the scallop shell in Botticelli's *Birth of Venus*.

Ironically, however, Harlow's real-life romantic affairs fizzled (and how!) more than they sizzled. "I thought it was awfully messy," she shrugged after her first intimate encounter at age sixteen. According to celebrity biographer Nigel Cawthorne, she laughed off a pass by Louis B. Mayer, MGM's head honcho, proclaiming that she'd sleep with him only if she thought she'd pass along an STD in the process. And certainly her months-long marriage (the second of three such short-lived liaisons) at twenty-one to Paul Bern, a studio executive literally twice her age, was enough to make a sex goddess look for an easier line of work. Despondent—or so many Hollywood historians conjecture—due to chronic impotence, Bern penned a brief suicide note to his sex symbol spouse ("You understand that last night was only a comedy," it read in part) and shot himself in the head.

Bright as she burned on the big screen, Harlow wasn't destined to linger long in the world, either. At the age of twenty-six, she died of kidney disease, leaving behind a flurry of unsubstantiated rumors, a few risqué quips ("I like to wake up feeling a new man," she told one reporter who inquired about her morning routine)—and a still-scorching celluloid image.

> *"No one ever expects a great lay to pay all the bills."*
> —JH

Harlow: Too hot for her hubby?

Ave Ava

*I*f the United States is a nation where poor boys have grown up to become President, it's also a nation where their female counterparts have been known to wind up as movie stars. To wit, the rags-to-riches saga of Ava Gardner, snugly ensconced between Rita Hayworth and Marilyn Monroe in the role of Great American Sex Symbol.

The barefoot daughter of a ne'er-do-well North Carolina tenant farmer, Gardner was plucked from obscurity (and an incipient secretarial career) in 1940, when an MGM scout spotted her photo in a relative's photography studio. "She can't act. She can't talk," concluded Louis B. Mayer when he saw the exquisite eighteen-year-old's screen test. "She's terrific." And so MGM groomed Gardner for stardom—courtesy of the studio, she took courses in drama, diction, physical fitness, and makeup application—and a star was what they got. Transformed into a temperamental diva with what one critic termed a "tigresslike quality of sexuality," Gardner made sixty-one films, attracted hordes of studly suitors, and is still considered by many to have been the most awesome-looking actress America has ever known.

She was not, however, considered the most talented—at least not by MGM, although the studio kept her under contract from 1941 to 1958. But her sex symbol status translated into big box office business, and MGM cast Gardner in one mediocre movie after another, knowing that her name (not to mention her face) guaranteed good ticket sales. Still, she made the most of the occasional opportunity to do more than simply decorate a film (most notably in *The Killers, The Night of the Iguana,* and *The Barefoot Contessa*), and was nominated for a Best Actress Academy Award for her performance in *Mogambo*.

As the press of the day made perfectly clear, Gardner's "tigresslike qualities" weren't

Gardner shows off her perfect profile

reserved for the silver screen alone. "When I lose my temper, honey," she admitted, "you can't find it anyplace." Stormily married to Mickey Rooney for several months and to musician Artie Shaw for a similarly brief interval, Gardner stole Frank Sinatra away from Nancy and remained Mrs. S for six tempestuous, tabloid-titillating years. Here's the homewrecker herself, setting backseat moralizers straight: "Some people say Liz [infamous mansteafer Elizabeth Taylor] and I are whores, but we are saints. We do not hide our loves hypocritically, and when we love we are loyal and faithful to our men."

Gardner never lost touch with Sinatra, who is said to have spent more than a million dollars on her medical bills during her final illness in the late 1980s. But following their divorce, she turned her shapely back on Hollywood gossip and took up residence in Madrid for several years. To the annoyance of neighbor Juan Perón, the exiled Argentinian dictator, she also took up with a succession of handsome but noisy-at-night matadors. In fact, the American star found herself so in sync with Spanish passions that she frequently flamencoed till dawn, tried her hand at bullfighting, and wrenched herself away from Madrid only when tax troubles made relocation prudent.

Gardner spent her final two decades in London, returning to the U.S. only to make the occasional film "strictly for the loot." But as you probably don't need to be told, her aversion to the American way of life was never a two-way street. Though the feisty film star passed on in 1990, a plethora of biographies, Web sites, and even the heavily-trafficked "Ava Gardner Museum" of Smithfield, North Carolina attest to her still-powerful pull on the American psyche.

"I'm one Hollywood star who hasn't tried to slash her wrists or take sleeping pills."

—AG

Cross My Heart

Huge hooters earned Jayne Mansfield the dubious title of "Miss United Dairies," not to mention an adulterous date with JFK. Lana Turner wasn't called "The Sweater Girl" because she had a closet full of couture knitwear. And even today, Raquel Welch is more noted for being "silicone from the knees up" (in the words of one Hollywood makeup man) than for her thespian skills.

In the entire breast-obsessed history of Hollywood, however, no chest has ever been quite so closely scrutinized as that of pneumatic knock-out Jane Russell. Never mind that her largesse wasn't limited to the anatomical sort (Russell was responsible for bringing some 43,000 European orphans to the U.S. in the wake of World War II, and overseeing their adoption). A titillating torso, not humanitarian qualities, made the swervy starlet an American household name.

In fact, Russell landed her first and most infamous screen role in 1940 solely due to her eye-catching thirty-eight-inch circumference. According to the discerning director Howard Hughes, only a gal with outsize garbanzos could convincingly portray the trollopy female lead in his forthcoming film, *The Outlaw*. And during the course of a nationwide bounty hunt, the sensitive *auteur* was simply bowled over by Russell's nineteen-year-old knockers.

Little did the sag-free starlet (a devout Christian who was only vaguely interested in an acting career at the time) suspect that the brouhaha about her bosom had only just begun. "We're not getting enough production out of Jane's breasts," Hughes carped when he viewed the daily rushes of *The Outlaw* (and no, he wasn't talking about milk). The next thing Russell knew, Hughes himself had personally whipped up a wacky 1940s version of the Wonderbra™, specifically designed to lift and separate her supremely photogenic flesh.

No one knows for sure whether the actress ever appeared on-screen in that much-ballyhooed bit of handiwork. According to at least one biographer, she simply made a few covert adjustments to her own low-tech brassiere, and the designing director (not to mention the public) never knew the difference. With or without benefit of Hughes' hydraulic expertise, however, Russell's décolletage didn't pass muster with the boob-phobic bureaucrats of the Hays office. Though *The Outlaw* was completed in 1941, it would take another two years—and eleven minutes of cleavage cuts—to satisfy the censors. And not for another half-decade would Hughes celebrate the film's general release—by hiring skywriters to etch a huge pair of breasts in the Hollywood skies.

In the end, of course, *The Outlaw* was an unmitigated commercial success, thanks in part to a series of salacious studio advertisements inquiring "What are the two reasons for Jane Russell's stardom?" But the leading lady's well-exploited bustline got better reviews than her rather flat (so the joke went) performance. And for years to come, Russell (who eventually achieved a degree of critical acclaim as Marilyn Monroe's brunette sidekick in *Gentlemen Prefer Blondes*) languished in the shadow of her own monumental measurements.

Contrary to what you might conjecture, however, religious Russell didn't think the less of herself for capitalizing on her amplitude. "I honestly feel sorry if *The Outlaw* publicity campaign was responsible for the young girls who decided that the only way to make it in show business was to shove out their bosom," she conceded in *My Path and Detours*, her 1985 autobiography. But, noted the still-stacked star (whose middle-aged mammaries were featured in many a brassiere commercial of the 1970s), "Christians can have big tits too."

> *"There are breast roles and there are nonbreast roles. For instance, when I was Stella in*
> A Streetcar Named Desire *on Broadway in 1988, I thought they were appropriate."*
> —Frances McDormand

NOT THE BREAST-KNOWN ACTRESS

A four-time Oscar nominee, Rosalind Russell was famed for her stage and screen roles in (and as) *Auntie Mame*. In the eyes of some, however, RR simply didn't measure up. "That isn't what I wanted," one autograph-seeker informed Russell when she saw how the celebrity had signed her name. "I wanted *Jane* Russell, the one with the big. . . ." But at this point, words failed the candid fan—though whether this was due to extreme delicacy or extreme disappointment, we cannot say for sure.

WHY MEN AND WOMEN WILL NEVER
BE BOSOM BUDDIES

"We must put brassieres on Joan Blondell and make her cover up her
breasts or we are going to have these pictures stopped in a lot of
places . . . . For Lord's sake, don't let those *bulbs* stick out."
—Top-drawer tycoon Jack Warner to producer Hal Wallis

"Here, hold my tits for me, will ya?"
**—"Oomph" girl Ann Sheridan, who found her studio-imposed
rubber falsies a heavy burden to bear**

"I presume you have a bust—show it."
**—Producer David Selznick, in a 1948 memo to
buttoned-up actress Ann Todd**

"Someone asked Marie McDonald if she minded being nicknamed
'The Body,' and she said that in Hollywood a girl doesn't
get very far being known as 'The Brain.'"
—The missile-shaped Jayne Mansfield

"She has a lovely bust. It's the right shape—it doesn't sag,
it doesn't droop, it isn't all distorted."
**—Stylist Richard Christian, via à vis the A-O.K.
anatomy of Stephanie Powers**

"When all that silly publicity was zooming in on Gina Lollobrigida's
and Sophia Loren's boobs, I was looking at their waists.
Perfect, tiny little waists!"
—Natalie Wood

"We must have naked breasts in this movie four times. I don't care how
you do it. I just want naked breasts."
—*Valley Girls* **producer Irving Azoff**
(to double-breasted director Martha Coolidge)

"The mammary fixation is the most infantile—and
most American—of the sex fetishes."
—**Molly Haskell, movie critic**

"The old boob question. You can't cast a girl unless she has them."
—**Director Bob Fosse, who once found Mariel Hemingway**
too flat to cast in sexy *Star 80*

"I didn't do it for the role. I didn't want to go through life being looked on
as just an athletic tomboy."
—**Mariel Hemingway, surgically inflated** *Star 80* **star**

Risqué Rita

There are bombshells, and then there are *bombshells*. As for Rita Hayworth—well, the auburn-haired actress was once deemed such a babe that her image decorated one of the first experimental atomic bombs. Hayworth's is not the happiest of stories; her girlhood was marred by incest, and Alzheimer's disease left her incapacitated in her fifties. Yet during a passionately-lived life anchored by those two tragic parentheses, she scorched an indelible mark across the screen of American culture. Touted by *Life* magazine as the nation's number one "Love Goddess" in 1947, Hayworth was known for her smoldering performances, sensational love affairs, and inspiring an epidemic of self-abuse among G.I.s who went gaga for her pinup photos.

The Brooklyn-born daughter of two professional dancers, Hayworth (or Margarita Carmen Cansino, as she was known at the time) began partnering her father onstage at the age of twelve—and, she later revealed, offstage as well. Shortly thereafter, she was "discovered" in a Tijuana night club, debuted on-screen at age seventeen, and promptly proceeded to languish as a B-movie bit player.

Eventually, a great dye job, a touch of electrolysis, and a WASPier sounding name transformed the former Ms. Cansino (and former brunette) into a highly marketable movie star. Not that she necessarily wanted to be one. In fact, Hayworth was almost allergic to the limelight, but, as she once explained, she simply didn't know how else to make a living. Riveting in a curve-clutching silver gown, the recent make-over crashed a Columbia Pictures casting meeting, and walked away with the starring role in *Only Angels Have Wings*. For the next several years, Hayworth sizzled through a series of landmark performances, most notably as a seductress in *Blood and Sand*, Fred Astaire's dance partner in *You'll Never Get Rich*, and an irresistible temptress in *Gilda*.

A truly explosive talent

If they'd had the chance, Hayworth's fans would certainly have paid top dollar to see her sizzle off-screen as well. Husband number one, Edward Judson, appreciated her primarily from the financial angle, but she proceeded to light quite a fire under her second spouse, the director Orson Welles. For years, her sexy escapades had Harry Cohn, head of Columbia Pictures, in such a jealous lather that he allegedly even bugged her dressing room. He might as well have spared himself the effort: when Hayworth was hot for a guy, she was hot, and when she wasn't—well, poor Mr. Cohn was stone out of luck.

Not so notorious playboy Aly Khan, the son of the Muslim spiritual leader Aga Khan. Hayworth scandalized the God-fearing citizens of several continents by romancing the not-quite-divorced Aly in hotspots all across Europe. When the affair proved all-engrossing, she scandalized Columbia, too, by giving notice that she was simply too tied up to work. Eventually, the high-profile pair did wed, but Aly just couldn't give up his womanizing ways, and the marriage was soon on the rocks. Hayworth returned to Hollywood flat broke (once upon a time, she had earned in the vicinity of $250,000 a year), with a new baby and without a beau... but she *still* wouldn't sleep with Cohn.

Subsequently cast chiefly in aging beauty roles (Hayworth was now all of thirty-nine), she embarked upon two more disastrous marital ventures before hanging up her veil for good. In the end, the "Love Goddess" had no trouble diagnosing her own recurrent romantic problem: "Every man I've known has fallen in love with Gilda and wakened up with me." The reason for her failing health and memory in her early fifties wasn't so clear, and many concluded that the star who once epitomized Hollywood-style eroticism had become a hardcore alcoholic. Hayworth died in 1987, after suffering for approximately two decades from Alzheimer's disease.

"All I ever wanted to be was myself."
—RH

The Myth of Marilyn

*I*t's not as though Hollywood had never produced a sex symbol before, for goodness sakes. From silent star Clara Bow on down, the film industry has colluded with film-goers in fixating on one erotic icon after another. Yet no other actress (and arguably no other woman) has ever seized the American imagination like Marilyn Monroe. Lovelorn foster child, radiant sex goddess, Presidential mistress, suicidal substance-abuser… as we all know, there are a million angles to Monroe's oft-told story—though angles, of course, were not what interested most of her fans.

Head-turning even in overalls, eighteen-year-old Monroe (born Norma Jean Mortenson) was working in a munitions factory when she caught the eye of an Army photographer. Soon to be divorced from her first husband, the then-brunette beauty got around, as they say—and so did the resulting pin-up photos. Monroe went on to become a model, and soon Hollywood was knocking at her door. Yet for a couple of years, the would-be movie star could barely get past the casting couch. As she later admitted, she sometimes resorted to trading sexual favors for food. "I was hungry," she explained, pressed to account for the nude calendar for which she posed at the time. Not that the proceeds could have kept her in groceries for long: Monroe netted $50 for baring her voluptuous bod, while the company that produced the calendar raked in $750,000.

Monroe appeared only fleetingly (albeit blondely) in her first film, *Scudda-Hoo! Scudda-Hay!* (1948)—the remainder of her scenes wound up on the cutting room floor. But her 1950 performance in *The Asphalt Jungle* resulted in an avalanche of fan mail. And breathless, babe-a-licious performances in several subsequent films—among them *Gentlemen Prefer Blondes* (1952), *How To Marry A Millionaire* (1953), *The Seven Year Itch* (1955)—made her into a genuine sex goddess. Of course, that impromptu City Hall marriage to Joe DiMaggio didn't exactly tarnish her image. "We haven't lost a star; we've gained a center fielder," exulted one Twentieth Century-Fox executive when he heard that the news. But DiMaggio had a hard time handling his bride's sexpot image, and the merger lasted only nine months.

Monroe, of course, had her own frustrations about being the source of so much prurient fascination. "If I'm going to be a symbol of something, I'd rather have it sex than some of the other things they've got symbols for," she conceded. Still, she yearned to do more in her movies than wiggle, pout, and demonstrate the erotic appeal of subway gratings. Then as now, "bombshell" was usually considered synonymous with "bimbo," and Monroe was mocked rather than applauded when she huffed out of Hollywood to study at the Strasbergs' Actors' Studio in New York. Yet upon her return, she made *Bus Stop* (1956), considered by many to be her finest film. Her act of defiance also gave her the leverage to negotiate a much more favorable contract with Twentieth Century-Fox. In addition, it afforded her the opportunity to mingle with a more intellectual crowd (Albert Einstein, believe it or not, was one of the fantasy object's own fantasy objects), and to meet her third and patently mismatched husband, the playwright Arthur Miller.

As for the seamier side of Monroe's life, most of us can recite the whole heartbreaking story in our sleep. The drink and the drugs, the abortions and the miscarriages, the compulsive couplings with Kennedys and co-stars, her tragic and controversial overdose at thirty-six—all are part and parcel of the Myth of Marilyn. And as biographers as disparate as Norman Mailer and Gloria Steinem have demonstrated, there's a message for everyone (though not, it seems, the same message) in this fabled star's still-haunting story.

> *"I don't want to make money. I just want to be wonderful."*
> —MM

Monroe in Movie Star mode

9¹/₂ *Piques*

Silent star Mary Pickford owned that ritzy piece of property known as Pickfair. Actress Marion Davies shared San Simeon, the costly castle-cum-tourist-attraction by the sea, with William Randolph Hearst. But only Kim Basinger, the siren who epitomizes late-twentieth-century sex appeal, personally purchased an entire town, hoping to turn it into a theme park. Worth $20 million to the movie star, Braselton, Georgia (population 418) had the added advantage of abutting, Basinger bragged, "the fields where I learned oral sex." (And here you thought fun-for-the-whole-family entertainment didn't get any better than Disneyland . . .)

Born in 1953, the beauty with the bee-stung lips not only obtained outside tutoring in the lingual skills, but went on to matriculate at the University of Georgia. Before she was old enough to vote, Basinger had also achieved a few ultra-'70s milestones—Breck girl, *Playboy* centerfold, *Charlie's Angels* appearance—that might have satisfied a less ambitious lady's quest for fame. But not *this* blonde bombshell, who debuted in the film *Hard Country* in 1981, spawned a nationwide craze for sexy refrigerator raids with her steamy performance opposite (and under, and so on) Mickey Rourke in *9½ Weeks*, and gave growing boys a whole new reason to appreciate *Batman*.

"I'm a highly, highly, highly creative human being," Basinger has said. "I write scripts constantly. I run my own production company." In fact, this chronic career-hopper once even cut an album titled *The Color of Sex*, though we can't swear the name wasn't influenced by a certain purple-loving artist formerly known both as Prince and as Basinger's beau.

But the buzz is that Basinger can also be a hard-to-work-with human being. A mondo pain in the pants on the set of *The Marrying Man* in 1991, she didn't win any popularity contests by cancelling rehearsals, criticizing the comedic sensibility of pre-eminent

Does this diva deserve the D-word?

scriptwriter Neil Simon, or spontaneously taking off to visit her psychic—in Brazil. "You can have diva behavior, but you've got to back it up with more than *hair*," groused one member of the *Marrying Man* crew. But Basinger (like self-described "bitch" Bette Davis before her) will brook no talk of the D-word. "You know what . . . difficult means? It means I'm a woman and I can't be controlled," bristles the—hmmm, easygoing? actress.

Call it a prima donna attitude or call it a strong sense of self-worth—either way, it landed the Georgia go-getter in legal trouble in the early 1990s. Here's the basic story: after verbally agreeing to star in *Boxing Helena* as a woman whose lover literally whittles her down to size, Basinger suddenly changed her mind. Well, no wonder she didn't want to do the film—in our opinion, Holly Hunter's severed digits in *The Piano* provide as much woman-as-symbolic-amputee shtick as anyone needs (or wants) to see. But producer Carl Mazzocone was so P.O.'d by his no-longer-leading lady's poor manners (he'd have been satisfied, he claimed, with a simple "I'm sorry") that he hauled her into court, and emerged with a multi-million dollar judgment in his favor. As a result, Basinger was forced to file for bankruptcy, and there, of course, went Braselton.

Real estate tycoon or no, however, Basinger (awarded a Best Supporting Actress Oscar for *L.A. Confidential* in 1998) and her self-esteem are here to stay. Scarcely mellowed by her marriage to fellow firecracker Alec Baldwin—as you may recall, Mr. Baldwin once clocked a paparazzi who snapped a shot of the couple's newborn child—Basinger simply turns a deaf (if dazzlingly beautiful) ear to her critics. As she once explained (or, more likely, expostulated): "I don't have time to be classified as difficult, and I don't have time to care."

"Women are cynical about being used as sex objects. Which is a shame,
because it's fun to use your sexuality."
—KB

A BRUSH WITH FAME

Poor Pablo Picasso (no beauty queen, he) had no choice but to use a paintbrush. Not so, however, fiftyish actress/artist Farrah Fawcett, who finds that her phenomenal naked corpus makes a fab tool for applying color to canvas. Fans of the former Charlie's Angel can check out her latest body of work in a 1997 *Playboy* video titled *All of Me*. Each art appreciator will have to determine for him/herself, however, whether the tawny-tressed one also eschews the concept of airbrushing.

Care to see my etchings?

3

Manic Monologuists

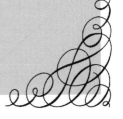

Dear Diary

*H*ormone-crazed teens are notorious for doing it. Anais Nin's whole life revolved around it. At this very moment, in fact, scores of misguided lovers are falling prey to this irresistible temptation. We're not speaking of illicit sex, of course, but of that infamous post-coital urge to run right home and record every last juicy detail (a drive, it seems, that many women find considerably more compelling than The Act itself)!

Few kiss-and-tell types, however, have ever been *quite* as enthusiastically indiscreet as Mary Astor, the much-loved leading lady of *Beau Brummel, The Maltese Falcon,* and dozens of other films from the early 1920s through the 1940s. "It was wonderful to f*** the entire sweet afternoon away," Astor (then married to the second of her four spouses, and the mother of one) gloated to her diary in 1935. "I don't know where George got his staying power!" A few pages later: "Once George lays down his glasses, he is *quite* a different man...we shared our fourth climax at dawn." Later still: "Ah, desert night—with George's body plunging into mine, naked under the stars...." And so on.

Needless to say, venereally-gifted George (aka George Kaufman, the Pulitzer Prize-winning playwright) was *not* Astor's husband. Dr. Franklyn Thorpe, however, was, and the discombobulated doctor nearly strangled himself with his stethoscope when he discovered this blow-by-blow account of his wife's hot-and-heavy sixteen-month affair. (Thorpe just happened to find the journal, incidentally, while rummaging through Astor's lingerie—but that, it would seem, is another story altogether, and no doubt an equally unsavory one.)

Confronted with her handwritten confession, Astor denied nothing. She flat-out refused, however, to give up those "naked under the stars" nights with her marathon man. (Hmm, wonder why?) Suffice it to say that the subsequent divorce and custody proceedings (in which Astor's journal, of course, served as the star witness) provided equal parts of personal pain and amusing tabloid fodder, and only by happenstance did Astor inhabit an age when an illicit affair was not a total show-stopper, career-wise.

As for the tell-tale diary, it was confiscated at the close of the legal process, remaining under lock and key for over fifteen years until court officials finally torched it in 1952. These upstanding citizens, surely, carried out that sober office with all due respect for the parties (not to mention the parts) involved. Not for a second, we imagine, were they tempted to commit the *second* oldest journal-istic sin in the book—perusing another person's private musings without a specific invitation to do so.

"You may say I did not *keep a diary."*
—George Kaufman (to reporters demanding details of the Astor affair)

WITHOUT ME, BABY, YOU'D BE NOBODY

Sad but true: selfless mother (or father) love sometimes flies right out the window when mondo chunks of cash are involved. According to Coral Amende, author of the titillating tome *Hollywood Confidential*, actresses Mary Astor, Gene Tierney, Paulette Goddard, and Veronica Lake were all sued for non-support by their parents. Along similar lines, Amende writes, Sophia Loren's papa was so peeved when she called him a cheapskate (well, words to that effect, anyway) that he charged his bella bambina with libel. Oh well. "When a child abruptly quadruples her family's income," Shirley Temple once noted, "some changes may be expected."

BEHIND EVERY GREAT MAN . . .

It's always touching when a famous-type guy acknowledges his gratitude to the lady who gave him life. But when it comes right down to it, the proud parents of celebrity offspring (and the indifferent ones, as well) are usually quite, quite capable of speaking for themselves . . .

Once an aspiring actress, Anna Hamilton never won an Oscar—let alone a memorable movie role. But George ("The Tan") Hamilton's mama truly deserved a medal (perhaps a *bronze* one) for her uplifting attitude. Still solicitous of her looks at seventy-something, Mother Hamilton signed up for improvements to her bosom, ignoring warnings that a lift could be lethal at her age. "Don't worry about that," she shrugged. "If the worst happens, you'll bury me topless."

In 1951, Karl Malden snared an Oscar for his supporting role in *A Streetcar Named Desire*. But Minnie Malden, the woman who spawned the star, also got off her share of good lines. Even in her final wheelchair-bound years, Mrs. Malden (who lived to the astonishing age of 104) was capable of wisecracking when her son asked how she felt. "With my hands, stupid," the centurian comedienne would reply.

Even his own mother found filming director William Wellman a bit too full of himself at times. Wellman was also apparently a bit too full of something else at the dinner party he threw for his maternal unit in 1945. Increasingly intoxicated as the evening progressed, he finally proposed a pompous toast to "that dear little old lady—my mother, who bore me." "Yes, son, and now you bore me," snapped his long-suffering parent.

MIRA, MIRA, OFF THE WALL

Mira Sorvino was sired in 1967 by nationally-known actor Paul Sorvino, collected her sheepskin (cum laude, no less) from Harvard in 1990, and acquired an Academy Award for Best Supporting Actress in Woody Allen's *Mighty Aphrodite* in 1996. Nonetheless, **Esquire** magazine reported, Mira Sorvino met a man at a party in 1997 who literally *did not know* who she was! Needless to say, Mira Sorvino did not hesitate to set him straight. "I'm Mira Sorvino, an actress!" she exclaimed. And, Mira Sorvino added helpfully, "You have embarrassed yourself more than anyone else could at this party. I've done fifteen movies and won an Oscar."

Self-assured Sorvino

SOME FRANK TALK ABOUT CLARK

Millions of moviegoers in the '30s and '40s swooned over, mooned after, and pined for matinee idol Clark Gable. "Any woman who is not attracted to him is dead," sighed actress Joan Blondell, while Marilyn Monroe broke out in goosebumps when he accidentally (so she said, anyway) brushed against her breast. But the sex symbol who starred in so many private fantasies (and a vast number of real-life acts as well) never considered himself a stud. "I do not want to be the world's greatest lover," declared "The King" (as he was known to legions of fans)—and evidently he got his wish. Not only did some of Gable's most prominent playmates consider his reputation as a Romeo overrated, but they didn't hesitate to say so—quite, quite frankly, my dear. . . .

> "If Clark had one inch less, he'd be 'the queen of Hollywood'
> instead of 'the king.'"
> **—Carole Lombard (Gable's third wife)**

> "Doing love scenes with Clark Gable in *Gone With the Wind* was not
> that romantic. His dentures smelled something awful."
> **—Vivien Leigh**

> "His ears were too big. Clark wasn't a good dancer either, all feet."
> **—Thelma Lewis (Gable's first girlfriend)**

> "He wasn't a satisfying lover. I often tried to
> distract him from the bedroom."
> **—Joan Crawford (Gable's mistress for many years)**

"I chewed gum, and during takes I would poke a wad up next to my teeth. But once, Clark kissed me too forcefully. When he drew back, we were attached by a ribbon of sticky gum! I shrieked with laughter as Clark glumly picked the gum from his teeth."
—**Lana Turner**

"She'll be blabbing it all over town the next day what a lousy lay I am."
—**Clark Gable (shrinking from a liaison with actress Lupe Velez)**

"God knows I love Clark, but he's the worst lay in town."
—**Carole Lombard**

"I guess I'll just have to practice more."
—**Clark Gable**

I REALLY *AM* YOUR BIGGEST FAN

Bette Davis knocked 'em dead when she gave a series of poetry readings in 1960. Scarcely had she taken the stage one evening when an elderly fan expired of a heart attack, and was dramatically removed from the theater. This discouraging development did not prevent the dearly departed's sibling, likewise attending the event, from remaining riveted to her seat. "I adored the performance," she gushed to Davis at the conclusion of the program. "And my sister would have too, if she hadn't died two hours ago!"

BETRAYED BY A KISS

Tongue-tied no more

As glamorously amoral as we may yearn to be, most of us simply don't have the time to trash our reputations (let alone our $1,000-a-night hotel rooms). Not so, however, in Movie-Star Land, where the dirty laundry flaps merrily in the breeze, and it by no means diminishes a star's cachet if his/her name comes up in a rousing session of kiss-and-tell. Well, not *usually*, anyway. More than a decade after her 1986 role opposite hunky Harrison Ford in *The Mosquito Coast*, actress Helen Mirren belatedly besmirched Ford's sexy image by dissing his onscreen smooches. Indeed, claimed the babbling Brit, every other actress to whom she mentioned the bummer busses agreed that "he couldn't do it with me either!" But the worst was yet to come. "He's probably not very good offscreen either," surmised Mirren the Mouth. Hmmm...any Florence Nightingales out there willing to tutor the he-man heart-throb in remedial osculatory techniques?

To Put It Bluntly...

Since jet-setting actress Merle Oberon left a hefty chunk of cash to the Motion Picture Country House and Hospital when she died in 1979, the grateful recipients named a rose garden after her. But during her lifetime, the acid-tongued dough donor didn't always come up smelling—or sounding—especially sweet.

Oberon's initial stage name, Queenie O'Brien, didn't suggest anything too top-drawer, either. In the '30s and '40s, however, the bicontinental beauty was in demand as a leading lady on both sides of the Atlantic, and her role in *Dark Angel* earned an Academy Award nomination in 1935. Nor was her early success any flash in the pan—Oberon didn't make her final film, *Interval*, until 1973 (intriguingly, actor Robert Wolders, who played her much-younger lover in that film, later became her much-younger spouse in real life). But the lines for which we really remember much-married, much-divorced, and, according to some critics, only moderately-talented Merle were her own outrageous stinkers—as often delivered, it might be noted, in the bedroom as on the set.

According to gossip columnist Sheila Graham, Oberon couldn't help gloating when a really *big* star landed in her boudoir. "Just imagine, I'm in bed with Jimmy Cagney!" she exclaimed in the midst of an intimate interlude with—yes, James Cagney. Though the remark was certainly accurate, Oberon's paramour wasn't bowled over by her keen powers of observation. "I hear it somewhat diminished his ardor," Graham noted.

Screenwriter Edwin Mayer, who knew Oberon during her six-year incarnation as Mrs. Alexander Korda, spouse of the prominent British director-producer, also got a taste of that hopelessly tactless tongue. "If you tell anyone about this," she supposedly hissed immediately after their adulterous act, "I'll tell my husband. He's more important than you and he'll ruin you."

Her role as the tragic heroine Cathy in *Wuthering Heights* (1939) found Oberon once again in bed—though this time as a rather lovely corpse. For whatever reason, however, actor David Niven (cast as Edgar) had a hard time with a script that called for him to dissolve in grief over her lifeless form. After several unsuccessful efforts to summon up tears, Niven finally resorted to the old menthol-in-the-eyes technique for jump-starting the sobs. Still no tears—though a viscous green substance suddenly began to flow from his nose. "Oh! How horrid!" quoth the ever-sensitive (and supposedly dead) movie star.

"If you don't have good stories to tell on your deathbed, what good was living?"
—Jennifer Tilly

THE PRINCESS AND THE PEE

Nature called, Jamie Lee Curtis responded, and there went her chance to meet Princess Diana, briefly (apparently *very* briefly) visiting the set of *Fierce Creatures* in London. So the American actress sat right down and wrote Diana a note of explanation. "I'm really sorry that I missed your visit," she informed the departed royal. "I've admired you for a long time, but I had to pee."

Oberon's lips were seldom sealed

"I'M SO F****** THRILLED"
(WHOOPI GOLDBERG, 1990)

For some, life didn't get any sweeter. For some, the evening reeked of sour grapes. But whether they really, really liked it, or really, really loathed it, not one of these assertive Academy Award attendees intended to shut up and smile…

Vanessa Redgrave didn't win any popularity contests in 1977. She did, however, win the Best Supporting Actress award—not, of course, that you'd have it known from the impassioned anti-Zionist speech she delivered in lieu of the standard thanks.

"The first thing that came to my mind was 'Did I or didn't I put on my girdle tonight?' Then I thought 'So what? Let it bounce.'" (Jane Wyman, Best Actress 1948)

"I just hope they pan the camera on me just once," Eileen Heckart remarked shortly before she was named Best Supporting Actress of 1972. "I paid a lot of money for this dress and I want my mother in Columbus, Ohio, to be able to see it."

"I deserve this." (Shirley MacLaine, Best Actress 1983)

Marlon Brando won the Best Actor award for 1972, but Apache activist Sacheen Littlefeather stole the show. According to the statement Littlefeather read on Brando's behalf, Tinseltown's poor "treatment of American Indians" made it impossible for him to accept the award. It later came out that the multi-faceted Ms. Littlefeather was synonymous with professional actress Maria Cruz and had won the title "Miss American Vampire" in 1970.

Sophia Loren celebrated her Best Actress award for 1961 by donating (not drinking) a pint of blood.

Without a doubt, the old Jane Fonda would have used the podium as a bully pulpit for her left-wing political views. But it was a kinder, gentler, and more physically fit Fonda who introduced the Best Picture segment in 1988 by urging the audience to view the nominated films "in a theater." On the other hand, the then-exercise entrepreneur noted, "You wanna watch videotapes, I know some terrific videotapes you can watch."

"I've had it. I want to be a full-time wife." (Susan Hayward, Best Actress 1958)

Beauteous in borrowed Mary McFadden, filmmaker Jessica Yu waxed candid on the subject of cash flow. "You know you've entered a new territory when you realize that your dress cost more than your film,"

commented the winner of the 1996 Best Documentary Short Subject award.

During the 1991 ceremony, one interviewer unwittingly put his foot in it by asking Whoopi Goldberg how she felt. "I've got my period," Goldberg shared.

Female contributions to film were lauded (well, kind of, anyway) at the annual festivities in 1992, the so-called "Year of the Woman." But *Feminine Mystique* author Betty Friedan, who just happened to be on hand for the hoopla, would have preferred a little less lip service. "It was worse than shallow," she reported. "It was contemptuous and patronizing. It had no basis in reality."

For different reasons, Ginger Rogers didn't think much of the "Year of the Woman" winging, either. In her day, as we all know, Rogers did everything Fred Astaire did—only backwards and in high heels. But at eighty-one, the happy hoofer had had it with heroics. After posing for a picture with sixty-six other women who had once won Oscars, Rogers revealed that she was required to sit on a hard box throughout the hour-long photo-shoot. "My derriere hurts like someone was beating me," she bitched.

"I need a drink." (Lila Kedrova, Best Supporting Actress 1964)

THE STORY OF O

Yep, Oscar really is all man. And lest the point escape us, America's most coveted 13¹/₂–incher even comes clutching that classic phallic symbol, the sword, in his tiny gold-plated hands. But although the Academy Awards were instituted in 1927, the Big O remained as nameless as a one-night stand until 1931, when a woman finally lifted the cloak of anonymity from the virile statuette.

Which woman, however, is a matter of dispute. One school holds that it was Margaret Herrick, then a secretary at the Academy of Motion Picture Arts and Sciences (later the Academy's executive director) who noted that the golden boy "reminds me of my uncle Oscar." (Conveniently, there just happened to be a columnist on hand to record and disseminate the remark.) Others claim that the name was coined by two-time Academy Award winner Bette Davis to honor her first husband, Harmon Oscar Nelson. But whatever the provenance of the prosaic moniker, it's as true today as it was in 1931: not even Warren Beatty can top good old Oscar's status as the guy that *every* American movie star dreams of taking home.

The Naked Truth(s)

Julia Roberts may be toothsome, but not having been born until 1967, she's scarcely long in the tooth. So it's certainly understandable if commitment isn't currently this sweet young thing's *thing*. Besides, Lyle's (and Kiefer's, and Jason's, and, well, you get the picture) ex didn't pull down a cool $12 million for *My Best Friend's Wedding* because she's so amazingly *set in her ways*. What *does* boggle the mind, however, is not the number of nabobs with whom The Pretty Woman has presumably gotten naked, but the number of (usually contradictory) opinions she's managed to voice on the subject of nakedness itself.

ROBERTS' RULE OF NUDITY: TAKE 1

On one occasion when Roberts held forth on the subject of unadorned flesh, she came across like a latter-day Marilyn Monroe, all faux innocence and fluttering lashes. "I only put clothes on," she explained, "so I'm not naked when I go out shopping." (Presumably not for clothes.)

ROBERTS' RULE OF NUDITY: TAKE 2

At another point, Roberts decided that nudity (hers, anyway) was a big no-no. "When you act with your clothes on, it's a performance," she opined. "When you act with your clothes off, it's a documentary. I don't do documentaries."

ROBERTS' RULE OF NUDITY: TAKE 3

When Roberts started to shiver while shooting an outdoor water scene in *Sleeping with the Enemy* (1991), she decreed that the underlings on the crew should strip to their underwear so they could share her pain (though not, of course, her salary).

The (sometimes) buff beauty

ROBERTS' RULE OF NUDITY: TAKE 4

Most recently, Roberts appears to have attained a profound new perspective on this perennially perplexing topic. "Why," she inquired soulfully of a *T.V. Guide* interviewer in June 1977, "do we all have to be naked to get along?" Rodney King couldn't have said it better...or could he?

THE AUDIENCE IS LISTENING

Though the romantic 1924 film *Three Weeks* was silent, leading lady Aileen Pringle wasn't. This created problems when lip-reading members of the Deaf and Dumb Society caught Pringle's comment as her lover lifts her in his arms. "If you drop me, you #$**X*!, you X#$%, I'll break your neck!" she enunciated.

THE BALD EGO

Though millions of American women are plagued by low self-esteem, it's scarcely the malady of choice for celebrities. To wit, the self-satisfied remarks of some stars who are (or were) vigilant about getting enough Vitamin Me...

"When I look at myself, I am so beautiful, I scream with joy."
—**Maria Montez**

"There's nothing better than to know I can be taking a bath at home and at the same time someone is watching me in Brazil."
—**Barbra Streisand**

"I'm magnificent. I'm five feet eleven inches and I weigh one hundred thirty-five pounds, and I look like a racehorse."
—**Julie Newmar**

"When I'm working well, I like to think I'm doing God's work."
—**Faye Dunaway**

"I look fabulous for my age."
—**Jane Fonda**

"I'm *fiercely* intelligent."
—**Sharon Stone**

"My butt! It fascinates me...I like it so much that when I dance, I'm always looking back at it."
—**Tori Spelling**

"I'm more subtle about how I demand to be worshipped."
—**Glenn Close**

CUT!

As far as an adoring public was concerned, Cecil B. De Mille was the guy who made epic movies. To those who actually worked with him, however, De Mille was known as the guy who made epic monologues. Worse yet, the great director demanded his entire cast's rapt attention during his lengthy lectures—or else. On one occasion, he noticed an extra chatting with her neighbor during one of his marathon soliloquies, and sarcastically inquired if she'd like to share her whispered comments with *everybody* on the set. No problem, shot back the brazen miscreant, who proceeded to broadcast her remark via microphone. "I was just asking my friend when was that old, bald-headed son-of-a-bitch gonna let us have lunch!"

4

Reprobate Role Models

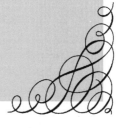

Hollywood Hay-zing

P ictures were still silent in 1922. But the bumper crop of Hollywood scandals that erupted that year (among them the implication of starlets Mabel Normand and Mary Minter in a bizarre murder) were a little harder to hush up. Fearful that God-fearing Americans would start boycotting the movies (or that Uncle Sam would start regulating them), Hollywood's major moguls concluded that it was time for the film industry to start policing itself.

Headed by one Will H. Hays (whose relevant work experience included serving on President Warren Harding's also-scandal-racked cabinet), the newly-formed Motion Picture Producers and Distributors of America, Inc. (MPPDA) set about polishing the tarnished image of Tinseltown. Henceforth, it was decreed, movies would essentially be suitable for screening in convents, monasteries, and kindergartens. As for actresses and actors who made headlines for the wrong reasons—well, anyone who breached the brand-new morals clause in her contract would soon be looking for a new line of work.

Not until a tidal wave of conservatism swept across the nation in the early 1930s, however, did the MPPDA impose the Draconian list of film industry rules, regulations, and sometimes creatively-circumvented howlers that became known as the Hays or Production Code. From now on, films would depict only "correct standards of life"—and the circumstances under which silver screen staples such as sex, crime, and booze-fests could be construed as "correct" were few indeed. (Not so religion and "national feelings," which the Code decreed would be treated "respectfully"—if not with outright reverence.)

Although no one would call the Production Code a real knee-slapper, it's difficult today to see how anyone could take its provisions (especially the chivalrous/chauvinist

Marilyn really had the Hays boys going

ones) altogether seriously. Not only were the words "broad," "chippie," "slut," "tart," or "whore" never to be uttered onscreen, for example, but the obscure "cocotte," too, was now persona (or noun) non grata. Also specifically verboten were humorous anecdotes about farmer's daughters. This, of course, must have come as a great relief to many a sensitive Midwestern miss, and we presume that not a soul dared to snicker when *The Farmer's Daughter*—the title, that is—rolled across the screen in 1947.

It's hard to say who the Hays Office intended to protect (and from what) with the provision that "Scenes of actual childbirth, in fact or in silhouette, are never to be presented." In any event, scenes of actual *non*-childbirth didn't cut it, either: in the 1949 film *Beyond The Forest*, Bette Davis wound up visiting a psychiatrist's office instead of the originally-scripted abortion clinic. But surely few movie-goers, whatever their stance on reproductive matters, shared head censor Joseph Breen's contention that *From Here to Eternity* would have been a better picture if only Deborah Kerr had thought to throw a "beach robe or some other type of clothing" over her swimsuit prior to that famous smooch in the sand.

Hollywood runneth over with creative thinkers, however, and Hays' prosaic henchmen were ill-matched against individuals whose entire careers were based, when you got right down to it, on making up plausible stories. Even Marilyn Monroe, an actress seldom celebrated for outsize cerebral capacity, managed to stymie the censor bent on snipping a scene in *Let's Make Love* (1960) because Monroe's "horizontal" pose implied incipient hanky-panky. "So what?" cooed the great love goddess. "You can do that standing up." And so the scene was preserved in its pristine non-vertical format.

As you might imagine, self-made sex symbol Mae West, a perennial target of the Hays Office, wasn't the type to take it lying down, either. Over time, censors tried to excise numerous vintage Westianisms ("I wouldn't let him touch me, even with a ten-foot pole"; "Is that a gun in your pocket, or are you just glad to see me?") from her films. On other occasions, her best lines were simply amended to delete the dirt—and as much of the humor as possible.

But when the Hays Office brought in an on-set morals monitor during the filming of *Belle of the Nineties* in 1934, the "Queen of Sex" could take it no more. West's wit wasn't the only wicked thing about her: she quickly concocted a story about a kidnapping scare which made it necessary for her to hire several hunky helpers to protect her. The "babysitter" was fit to be tied when West hung a "Do Not Disturb" sign on her dressing room door and disappeared inside—along with the phalanx of physically-fit gentlemen who were (wink, wink) guarding her precious body.

Of course, West had a certain reputation to uphold, and she was the first to protest (or pretend to) when the Production Code gave way in 1968 to the kinder, gentler "alphabet soup" system of rating films. "If a picture of mine didn't get an 'X' rating, I'd be *insulted*," the empress of innuendo now claimed—but of course that was just her persona talking (and not, for example, her financial advisor). It was also West who famously said, "It isn't what I do, but how I do it. It isn't what I say, but how I say it and how I look when I do it and say it." Her words (not to mention her works) stand today as one of the most eloquent statements ever made about the folly—indeed, the futility—of attempting to legislate art.

Jail-House Frock

The overwhelming majority of American women wound up behind bars (or deserved to) during the early 1930s—at least, that's the impression you might get from that period's bumper crop of girl-gone-wrong films. In theater after theater, gorgeous gun molls, unrepentant hookers, or those ever-popular evil lesbians glowered down from their big-screen cells, titillating audiences and giving Tinseltown moguls a thrill every time they counted the box office receipts.

Most of these fallen-angel genre films, of course, sprang from the fertile imaginations of writers whose personal experience with hard time was having to rewrite the script again. Not so, however, Warner Brothers' 1933 blockbuster, *Ladies They Talk About*, based on a script by bona fide jailbird Dorothy MacKaye.

Born in Scotland in 1903, Dorothy was just another stage-struck seventeen-year-old when she hooked up with fellow actor (and future husband) Ray Raymond in the cast of a Broadway show. In the mid-1920s, Mr. and Mrs. Raymond, who planned to become Mr. and Mrs. Movie Star, made their mark on Hollywood by singing and dancing in an experimental short subject with an audio track. (*The Jazz Singer*, the world's first non-silent feature, came out a few months later.)

Audible vaudeville was nothing, however, compared to the kind of history the couple made in April 1927, when Raymond got into a head-slamming scrap with actor Paul Kelly. Right was on Raymond's side (Kelly's trysts with Dorothy were the talk of the town) but might most definitely was not. Suffice it to say that hubby wasn't looking too perky when his wandering wife put him to bed; by morning, he had fallen into a coma. Two days later, Raymond was dead, Dorothy's reputation was in tatters, and lover-boy Kelly's future as a free man didn't look promising.

Dorothy did her best to solve the problem—at her insistence, the examining physician reported that acute alcoholism, not acute fisticuffs, was responsible for Raymond's untimely demise. But the story didn't wash with the cops, and Kelly and MacKaye both ended up in San Quentin—he for manslaughter, she for feloniously concealing facts concerning the cause of her husband's death. From Kelly's point of view, it must be said, the verdict may not have been as painful as his trial: he had to endure hearing his love letters to Dorothy read aloud in court, including one passionate masterpiece he had penned in pig Latin.

Ever the busy bee, Dorothy took advantage of her stint in stir to hone her professional skills. She scribbled herself notes about the details of other inmates' lives and crimes, founded a drama club, and, having the benefit of a captive audience, even tried her hand at directing. If nothing else, those penitentiary performances were definitely one-of-a-kind: for one killer production, Dorothy cast only convicted murderers.

Paroled after a year for good behavior, Dorothy worked the ex-con gig for all it was worth in *Women in Prison*, her well-received (though not very imaginatively titled) stage play. Indeed, her script was so strong that Warner Brothers was able to get *two* movies out of it—*Ladies They Talk About* and *Lady Gangster*, a 1942 remake. (It was also so strong that the Hays Office was able to get several feverish sex scenes out of it.)

And speaking of lurid lust—yes, Dorothy MacKaye, the jail-yard bard, and Paul Kelly, the pig Latin poet who offed her old man, were wed in 1931. And they say that rime-cay doesn't ay-pay, eh?

> *"Whatever has been done is done—but there is still a future for us."*
> —DM

You Great Big Beautiful Molls

O ften cast as a leading lady in the 1930s and '40s, Wendy Barrie won rave reviews as the ill-fated Jane Seymour in *The Private Life of Henry VIII*. Apparently, the native Brit liked her real-life liaisons on the dangereuse side as well. Affianced, during the course of her U.S. film career, to notorious mobster Benjamin "Bugsy" Siegel, Barrie risked her reputation and her career for love of her Mafia man. On one occasion, she even arranged to rendezvous with the gangster while he was supposedly in the slammer on murder charges. (Somehow, Bugsy had finessed his way out of the hoosegow for some emergency dental work, and—well, you know the drill.)

Bright as their passion burned, however, Barrie and Bugsy parted ways before they were legally wed. But at least Bugsy still had the consolation of his career. Not so Barrie, who found precious few parts tossed her way owing to her outré underworld affair. Ironically, the axed actress (who died in 1978 at the age of sixty-five) finally wound up as one of T.V.'s first talk show hosts—a gig that would certainly have put the fear of God (or of gab) in the close-mouthed Family man.

Virginia "Sugar" Hill, Bugsy's next Hollywood (by way of Alabama, Chicago, and New York) gal pal, was no more a Doctor of Dental Science than her predecessor. She did, however, have her stuff down cold when it came to oral hygiene. In fact, the so-called "Queen of the Mafia" once gave head hoodlum Charles Frischetti a public sample of her services—right in the middle of an absolutely "mobbed" Christmas party. As you might imagine, this little performance didn't go over big with the females of La Famiglia, who promptly exited the premises en masse. But Virginia "Flaunt It If You've Got It" Hill couldn't have cared less. "I'm the best damn c***sucker in Chicago and I've got the diamonds to prove it," she boasted. (Well, sometimes she did, and sometimes she didn't: when a guy fell out of Hill's graces, she retaliated by flushing his gems.)

Nice as she found the ice, however, Hill was no mere gold-digger: she wanted to be a starlet, too. Whether she put a bug in Bugsy's ear or whether she simply "ingratiated herself to Sam Goldwyn," as Hollywood biographer Kenneth Anger puts it, no one knows for sure. But by hook or by crook, the finest fellatrix in urban Illinois wangled her way into sharing the screen with Barbara Stanwyck and Gary Cooper in 1941's aptly-titled *Ball of Fire*. (Hence the odd spectacle of bad, bad Bugsy Siegel, Hill's sleazeball steady, mixing it up with movie stars at the film's premiere.)

Believe it or not, the Mafia moll went on to make quite a stir in Tinseltown's tonier social circles. Actor Robert Stack wasn't the only Hollywoodite who went a bit gaga when he noticed that the diamond-bedecked blonde "carried a roll of bills that would choke a horse." And according to gossip columnist Hedda Hopper, Hill (who may or may not have learned more sophisticated party tricks since her glory days in Chi-town) threw some of "the swingingest parties in town."

But the c***sucker and the criminal (played, by the way, by real-life lovers Annette Bening and Warren Beatty in the 1991 film *Bugsy*) weren't destined to reign as Hollywood's fast-living fun couple forever. In June 1947, Bugsy was lounging by the window of Hill's chi-chi Beverly Hills home when he bought the farm in classic gangland style, the bullet-riddled victim of a sharpshooter with a major financial grudge. But life certainly went on for his rare gem of a girlfriend, who was, at the very moment of Bugsy's death, having the time of her life doing Europe with a filthy rich young Gaul—and, we bet, racking up rocks like crazy.

> *"Is that a gun in your pocket, or are you just happy to see me?"*
> —Mae West

The Three Faces of Evil

When the popular director William Desmond Taylor was mysteriously murdered in his Hollywood mansion on February 2, 1922, the names of no fewer than nineteen possible perpetrators were published in periodicals across the country. A certain "Drug-Crazed Film Queen" made *everybody's* short list. And hordes of pathological liars leaped on the bandwagon, eagerly misconfessing to firing the bullets that proved fatal to the forty-four-year-old "Gentleman Director." Despite a plethora of potential suspects, however, police were unable to come up with a compelling case against anyone, and the murder remains unsolved to this day.

Investigators *did*, however, manage to get the goods on two well-known female film stars—plus one of their very own mothers—implicated in a lurid, possibly lethal love quadrangle with Taylor. And when John Q. Public learned how these femmes fatales spent their spare time (let's just say that their hobby wasn't knitting), all hell broke loose. By the time the dust cleared, America's movie moguls had come up with the mondo P.R. ploy known as the Hays Office to firm up film industry morals, and the halcyon days when Hollywood types could let it all hang out were nearly over. Following, the skinny on the three Eves who (with a little help from their boozing, using, or outright perverted peers) brought down the curtain on Eden…

1: The Cokehead Comic

"I like to pinch babies and twist their legs," deadpanned Mabel Normand when a reporter asked the inevitable tedious question about her hobbies. "And get drunk."

Of course, the response was a put-on. What Normand *really* liked to do was white, powdery, and potentially extremely destructive to a working girl's career. Nonetheless, the antic genius of silent comedy (who succumbed to T.B. at thirty-six) racked up some awesome professional accomplishments during her frenzied, flamboyant life. An artist's model at thirteen, a film actress at sixteen, the leading comedienne of Keystone Pictures at twenty, co-founder of the Mabel Normand Feature Film Company, sometime stunt-woman and a frequent (though often uncredited) director...Ever-so energetic Normand did it all, despite a bad habit (supposedly acquired by snacking on coke-doctored peanuts) that eventually ran her two grand a month.

It's not quite true that Charlie Chaplin stole his best lines from Normand, since during the celebrated silent years of his career, the diminutive pantomimist didn't, of course, have any. But according to some, Chaplin certainly picked up a trick or two (or a zillion) from the zany Keystone colleague who directed him in at least five different films. "A study of [Normand's] films, made before Chaplin came to this country," notes Raymond Lee in *Movie Memories*, "shows entire routines, gestures, reactions, expressions, that were later a part of Chaplin's characterizations."

Oh, well. "Behind every great man," as the saying goes (or should), "there's an underappreciated woman." To be perfectly fair, however, Normand also got behind some pretty mediocre guys, among them bachelor-boy William Desmond Taylor, the unsung Warren Beatty of the 1920s. Unfortunately for Normand, she just happened to be one of the two super-star sweeties who (apparently unbeknownst to one another) visited womanizing WDT the night of his death. And when police arrived the next morning, Normand was already on the scene, searching for some very private love letters she had written to the deceased. But evidence of the liaison was impossible to conceal—and as soon as the newshounds started nosing around, stories about Normand's interest in illicit substances were also impossible to suppress.

"It was a perfectly innocent coincidence that I was the last person to see Bill Taylor alive," Normand claimed, and investigators concluded that she was telling the truth. (Which was more than "Bill Taylor"—posthumously discovered to be one William Dean-Tanner, a fugitive husband and deadbeat dad—had apparently been able to do.) As far as the public was concerned, however, America's favorite funny woman was guilty of bad behavior, if nothing else, and moviegoers boycotted her latest feature, *Suzanna*, in droves. A few months later, the fatal shooting of millionaire Cortland S. Dines—with a pistol that was said to belong to Normand—delivered the coup de grace to her brief but brilliant career.

2: The Faux Virgin

Born in 1902, accomplished actress Mary Miles Minter was not yet twenty years old when director William Desmond Taylor (with whom she had often worked) turned into a corpse. Even so, she already had a decade of on-camera experience under her corset—all of it, of course, in the pure-as-the-driven-snow roles that befit her tender years.

Minter displays her maidenly charms

Who knows—perhaps this impressionable innocent appeared in one too many films with titles like *Beauty and the Rogue* or *The Amazing Imposter*. For concealed within one of Taylor's pornographic volumes titled (oh, the irony) *White Stains*, police discovered a declaration of love for the dead director—penned on pink stationery in Miss Minter's still-girlish hand. Nor was there any mistaking the significance of the pink silk nightgown, embroidered with the monogram MMM, that cops found hanging in Taylor's closet. Yes, it turned out, the pink-loving paragon of maidenly virtue had visited the deceased at his home on the evening of February 2. And yes, she admitted, she had "loved him deeply and tenderly, with all the admiration a young girl gives to a man with [his] poise and position."

As though she had not already performed enough services for her poised paramour, Minter managed to make an unforgettable affair out of Taylor's funeral, too. After bending to kiss the lips of the corpse, she made the startling announcement that it had responded by whispering "something ... [that] sounded like 'I shall love you always, Mary.'"

As it turned out, Minter would be haunted by Taylor's ghost for the rest of her life. The juicy details of that suave (and apparently sleep-deprived) Lothario's last action-packed evening on earth made fine artistic fodder for novelists and filmmakers over the years, and Minter eventually initiated an unsuccessful lawsuit against CBS for portraying her as a suspect in the crime. As for her acting career, it vanished along with her virginal image, and she never made another movie after the 1923 film titled, appropriately enough, *The Trail of the Lonesome Pine*.

3: Mom From Hell

*I*f Dante had lived in Hollywood, he'd have reserved an extra circle of hell for that parasitic breed of stage mothers who live off the sweat of their young. For a hardcore case like Charlotte Shelby, the pistol-packing parent of faux virgin Mary Minter, life in prison might also have been appropriate. Or so surmised the now-deceased MGM director/amateur sleuth King Vidor, who dredged up some fascinating dirt about the Taylor murder mystery for a proposed film in 1967.

Described by biographers as "greedy" and "vicious," Shelby was that one-in-a-million mama whose little darling really did make it big in the pictures—at the precocious age of ten. As an added bonus, Shelby evidently also got to meet lots of handsome Hollywood men during the course of her child's career. Among them was William Desmond Taylor, with whom she—like so many others before her—allegedly conducted an affair. So far, so good—not to mention *so* rich. But when Shelby discovered that Taylor was also "involved" with her now-nineteen-year-old daughter, the whole picture, according to Vidor, started to look less pretty.

Maybe Shelby was miffed because her little girl was no longer entitled to a white wedding (though pink, it seems, was not entirely out of the question). Maybe she was steamed because she understood that Minter's money-making potential hinged on an image of childish chastity. Or maybe she was simply outraged (and who wouldn't be?) at her lover's sleazy betrayal. But since Shelby was never charged with the crime, it must have been mere coincidence that witnesses saw her getting in some target practice (with her pearl-handled .38 revolver) shortly before her double-dipping lover turned up with a pair of (.38) bullets lodged in his heart.

For whatever reason, Vidor (who was acquainted, as a young man, with major headline-makers in L'Affaire Taylor) never did get around to making his movie. But if you, like your ancestors in the rip-roaring '20s, simply can't get enough of this vintage Hollywood scandal, check out Sidney Kirkpatrick's 1986 non-fiction thriller, *A Cast of Killers*, which purportedly Reveals All of Vidor's insider dope on Shelby, Minter, Normand, et al.

WE'RE NO ANGELS

Coincidentally or not, American women tumbled off the Victorian pedestal right around the time silent films appeared on the scene. And as a random sampling of girl-gone-wrong movie titles over the years suggests, we haven't got a prayer in Hollywood of rising to those virtuous heights again...

DANGEROUS WOMEN

Ladies Love Danger (1935)

Granny Get Your Gun (1940)

Lady Gangster (1942)

Annie Get Your Gun (1950)

The Texan Meets Calamity Jane (1950)

This Woman is Dangerous (1952)

Lady of Vengeance (1957)

Bloody Mama (1970)

A Dangerous Woman (1993)

SCARY WOMEN

Lady Scarface (1941)

Cobra Woman (1944)

Kitten With a Whip (1964)

Who's Afraid of Virginia Woolf? (1966)

The Medusa Touch (1978)

Women on the Verge of a Nervous Breakdown (1988)

POSSESSED WOMEN

The Devil's Daughter (1915)

The She-Devil (1918)

The Blonde Vampire (1922)

Satan's Sister (1925)

The Woman From Hell (1929)

The Godless Girl (1929)

Madam Satan (1930)

The Devil is a Woman (1935)

The Devil and Miss Jones (1941)

The Witches of Eastwick (1987)

She-Devil (1989)

CRIMINAL WOMEN

Condemned Women (1938)

Girls of the Big House (1945)

Women's Prison (1955)

Reform School Girl (1957)

SCARLET WOMEN

The Unchastened Woman (1925)

Lady of the Night (1925)

A Woman of Affairs (1928)

The Scarlet Lady (1928)

The Shady Lady (1929)

Bad Girl (1931)

The Sin of Madelon Claudet (1931)

She Done Him Wrong (1933)

Ex-Lady (1933)

Outcast Lady (1934)

Naughty Marietta (1935)

Jezebel (1938)

They All Kissed the Bride (1942)

Dishonored Lady (1947)

The Imperfect Lady (1947)

Call Me Madam (1953)

Girl of the Night (1960)

Sex and the Single Girl (1965)

She's Gotta Have It (1986)

Seven Women Seven Sins (1988)

WILD WOMEN

Theodora Goes Wild (1936)

A Woman Rebels (1936)

Julia Misbehaves (1948)

. . . And the Wild Wild Women (1958)

She's Out of Control (1989)

JUST PLAIN NO-GOOD WOMEN

When A Woman Sins (1918)

Bad Sister (1931)

Fired Wife (1943)

Weird Woman (1944)

The Wicked Lady (1945, 1983)

Smash-Up, the Story of a Woman (1947)

The Notorious Landlady (1962)

5

Bad-Ass Beauties

Much Ado About Marlene

Depending on the biographer, the real Marlene Dietrich was either an exotic European glamour girl—or an apron-clad hausfrau with a baby on her hip and flour on her nose. She was a leggy beauty with a penchant for see-through gowns—or a mannish androgyne who favored slacks over sequins, thus setting the trend for women in trousers that endures today. She was a rakish female Casanova who boasted scores of lovers of both sexes—or an old-fashioned sort who preferred emotional liaisons to sexual ones, and impotent, nondemanding lovers to virile ones. But one thing we know for sure about Dietrich: she had a very active social life.

It was, of course, her indelible portrayal of a sleazy nightclub singer in Josef von Sternberg's 1930 classic, *The Blue Angel*, that transformed Germany's leading lady into an international star, and one of the hottest Hollywood properties around. And yes, we do mean *hot.* Signed to a contract with Paramount Pictures in the '30s, Dietrich was designated as that studio's sexy rival to MGM's enigmatic European import, Greta Garbo. But Dietrich had little interest in maintaining an aloof mystique à la "The Swedish Sphinx." "I want to be alone," Garbo supposedly said.* "I hate to be alone," shuddered Dietrich. She seldom was.

"In Europe," explained the world-class seductress (who had an "understanding" with Rudi Sieber, her spouse for more than five decades), "it doesn't matter if you're a man or a woman. We make love to anyone we find attractive." As indifferent to the marital status of her conquests as she was to their sex, Dietrich is said to have done the deed with the likes of Mercedes de Acosta, Burt Bacharach, Yul Brynner, Maurice Chevalier, Gary Cooper, Kirk Douglas, Douglas Fairbanks, Jr., Alberto Giacometti, Joseph P. Kennedy, Fritz Lang, Edward R. Murrow, Edith Piaf, Erich Maria Remarque, Jimmy

The mistress of androgynous allure

Stewart, John Wayne, and Michael Wilding...as well as plenty of plain old Toms, Dicks, and Harriets. (Somehow, though, poor Papa Hemingway failed to make Marlene's list—their relationship, she said, "was too special for that.")

After spurning a plea from Nazi agents to continue her career in her homeland, Dietrich was naturalized as a U.S. citizen in 1937 (and her movies suddenly become very verboten in Germany). But even her expressions of American patriotism during World War II tended to bear an erotic imprint. Awarded the Medal of Freedom for "meeting a grueling schedule of performances under battle conditions despite risk to her life," Dietrich served her adoptive country by boosting the morale of U.S. troops abroad and making anti-Nazi broadcasts in German. But according to one story, she was also personally reprimanded by President Roosevelt for the "prostitution technique" she employed to hawk war bonds in nightclubs (the enthusiastic entertainer boosted sales—among other things—by sitting on drunken patrons' laps).

According to Douglas Fairbanks, Jr., Dietrich was "a wonderfully unconventional lover." Kenneth Tynan may not have meant it as a compliment when he concluded that Dietrich "has sex without gender," but in certain circles, such remarks only added to her allure. "I will bring anyone you want to your bed," pleaded a desperate Mercedes de Acosta, who knew all about her fickle Angel's Achilles heel, when Dietrich's passion for the author waned. And though Dietrich died (at the age of ninety) in 1992, her reputation as a lover lives on today. As no less a libido-freak than Madonna put it, "I wouldn't mind having had an affair with Marlene Dietrich when she was young. Like, who wouldn't?"

*Later in life, Garbo would claim that she had actually said that she wanted "to be *left* alone." Dietrich didn't want to be *left* alone, either.

> *"In America [sex is] an obsession. In other parts of the world a fact."*
> —MD

A PRIMA DONNA'S PRIMER

In 1961, a surprisingly well-lettered celebrity spoke her mind (and, presumably, earned a hearty helping of royalties) in a tiny tome titled *Marlene Dietrich's ABC*. Not for the faint of heart or weak of constitution, Dietrich's romp through the consonants and vowels ranged from Analysis (and her disdain thereof) to Zabaglione (and her recipe therefor—yes, magnificent Marlene knew her way around the kitchen as well as the boudoir). Other red-letter items in the androgynous actress/author's alphabet:

CIGARETTES
"I started smoking during the war. I have kept
it up ever since. It keeps me healthy."

GENDER
"At the best of times gender is difficult to determine.
In language gender is particularly confusing."

STAGE FRIGHT
"I have no sympathy with actors trembling in the wings.
They have chosen acting as their profession; let them get on with it."

WHITE BREAD
"I cringe every time I see a child eating a sandwich made out of American
white bread. Give them whole wheat or rye bread if you love your children."

WILL
"It is almost impossible to put on paper what one would
want done after one is dead."

The Sounds of Silence

"**G**arbo Talks!" trumpeted advertisements for *Anna Christie,* the film that marked Greta Garbo's transition from silents to talkies. In real life, however, loquaciousness was scarcely the legendary actress's thing. Living proof of the dictum "less is more," Garbo seldom appeared in public and rarely granted interviews. In fact, the diva was even known to ban directors from her sets. "When people are watching, I'm just a woman making faces for the camera," she insisted. "It destroys the illusion."

Raised in poverty in Stockholm, Garbo made her screen debut at sixteen, when she appeared in *How Not to Dress,* a promotional film for the department store where she worked as a salesgirl. Eventually, the film led to her discovery by Mauritz Stiller, the famed Swedish director. When Stiller, in turn, was discovered by Louis B. Mayer and offered a Hollywood contract, he insisted on bringing his protégé along.

Though Mayer grumbled that a "fat girl" like Garbo would never go over big in the U.S., he was forced to eat his words (and offer her a more generous contract) when her first film, *The Torrent,* proved a smash success. Few, in fact, were as unimpressed by Garbo's subsequent ascent to superstar status as the actress herself. "I cannot see any sense in getting dressed up and doing nothing but tempting men in pictures," she once complained. And at the height of her fame in 1941, the so-called "Sarah Bernhardt of films" abandoned Hollywood without explanation, to be only seldom seen (much less heard from) again.

No one can say for sure why the woman who electrified audiences in classics like *Anna Karenina* and *Camille* guarded her privacy so jealously. According to one inventive theory, Garbo was cursed with an ultra-frequent menstrual flow, and she became a recluse to conceal the condition. Others claim that she shunned publicity to avoid

The empress of exquisite silence

exposure as a lesbian, making much of the fact that she left fiancé John Gilbert standing at the altar on what was to have been their wedding day. Louise Brooks claimed that the androgynous actress once made a pass at her while playing tennis (and if anyone could recognize an overture from half-a-court away, it was that scarlet silent star). And ubiquitous Hollywood bedmate Mercedes de Acosta names Garbo (along with her fellow European Marlene Dietrich) as a long-term lover in her memoirs.

But in the end, what matter if this enigmatic, understated, and hauntingly beautiful actress preferred to impersonate a clam on the subject of her personal life? Her work—twenty-four Hollywood films in all, many of them still mesmerizing today—speaks for itself. And as "The Swedish Sphinx" herself put it, "I give them everything I've got on the screen. Why do they try to usurp my privacy?"

> *"I always wanted to be the boss."*
> —GG

GARBO GAB

"Mystery? She may be thinking the most profound of thoughts. She may be wondering if her herring will be chopped properly for dinner."
—*Photoplay*, 1930

"[Garbo] is hermaphroditic, with the cold quality of a mermaid."
—**Tennessee Williams**

"She made a career out of a perfect profile and doing so few interviews that no way could she bore the public."
—**Yul Brynner**

"The gloomiest Scandinavian since Hamlet."
—**Nigel Cawthorne, Hollywood biographer**

"[Garbo] had this androgynous quality. Some of this was her being European, with that elegance, that aloof, almost royal quality. If she'd been American, I think the ladies in the audiences would have thought her sort of dykey. Oops!"
—**Gale Sondergaard**

"For her, and her alone, I could have been a lesbian."
—**Joan Crawford**

NAME DROPPERS

From Norma Jean to Marilyn, from Frances to Judy, from Barbara to Barbra—first on every budding starlet's shopping list, it seems, is a sleeker, sexier moniker. But there *are* exceptions to the rule . . .

What, you never heard of Marie Tisdale? Well, if it hadn't been for movie buff Marie, you might never have heard of Joan Crawford (born Lucille Le Sueur in 1904), either. The story goes that Louis B. Mayer loathed young Le Sueur's alliterative appellation—he thought it sounded like "sewer." (Interestingly, "Garbo" also reminded Mr. M of "garbage.") So in 1925, MGM sponsored a *Movie Weekly* magazine contest to come up with something more star-ish. Unfortunately, the winning entry, "Joan Arden," was already in use by an actress named—oh, don't tell me—Joan Arden, and so Ms. Tisdale's second-place suggestion, "Joan Crawford," won by default. The future Mommie Dearest did not, by the way, care one little bit for the way her classy new name resembled the word "crawfish."

Frances Ethel Gumm's illustrious career was launched at the age of two, when she warbled her way into her older sisters' singing act. Entertainer George Jessel, for whom the Gumms opened in 1931, claimed that he perceived an urgent need for a "cheerful and festive" new surname when he saw that the girls were billed as "The Glum Sisters." And voilá—a very diminutive Judy Garland, chock-full of sweetness, light, and diet pills.

"Whoopi"—as in "Whoopi Goldberg"—also smacks of the "cheerful and festive," no? Actually, the former Caryn Johnson revealed in her 1997 autobiography, she impulsively renamed herself after a Whoopi cushion during a bad bout of flatulence.

★ ★ ★

In 1938, mighty Louis "What's In A Name" Mayer decreed that Hedwig Kiesler, the va-va-voom actress from Vienna, needed a name that would "look good, like butter on hot corn." But the newly-created Hedy Lamarr (after *very* silent movie star Barbara La Marr, who O.D.'d on narcotics in 1926) had a hard time handling her secondhand John Hancock. How hard? Well, when Ms. Lamar—oops, make that Lamarr—signed the register at her first Hollywood hotel, she spelled her own name wrong.

★ ★ ★

Early in her Hollywood career, one now-legendary actress played absolutely true to type (or what her type would become, anyway) when she refused to lose her birth name as casually as another would-be glamour girl might shed a layer of baby fat. That would be, of course, the aspiring actress who successfully resisted all efforts to transform her into "Bettina Dawes." Nothing doing, said Bette Davis, and steadfastly refused to adopt the handle that sounded, to her ear, exactly like "Between the Drawers."

The Fabulous Baker Girl

"I would like to meet the woman who has the courage even to play my life story in a film," the legendary entertainer Josephine Baker remarked at the age of sixty-seven, as she approached the end of her spectacular, passionately-lived life. "I do not believe the woman exists who would have had the courage to have *lived* it as I have done."

Okay, so modesty (in either sense of the word) wasn't one of brazen Baker's more outstanding characteristics. Suffice it to say that the teenage runaway from a St. Louis slum didn't become the toast of Paris in the (and her) '20s by hiding her light under a bushel. In fact, there wasn't much that Baker, the first black entertainer to star solo in a Parisian revue, liked to keep under wraps.

A self-styled refugee from American racism, she expressed her love of liberté (sartorial and otherwise) during her very first performance at the famous Folies Bergère, shimmying across the stage in little more than a G-string fashioned from bananas. And when the audience *also* went bananas, Baker (who was billed only as a dancer) impulsively pulled out all the stops, mugging, scat-singing, and even leaping into a faux banana tree.

Thus began a decades-long love affair between performer and audience, during which la belle Baker acquired French citizenship, opened her own nightclub, starred in several films of the revue genre (with deliciously campy titles like *La Sirène des Tropiques* and *Princesse Tam Tam*), and finally became the highest-paid entertainer in Europe.

By her own account, Baker may also have been the most-laid. "I'm not immoral, I'm only natural," the rich and ravishing man-magnet maintained—and naturally, she did the deed with "thousands" of beaux she barely knew, and the odd belle or two as well. Like every diva since the Dark Ages, Baker also kept a large menagerie of exotic pets,

Baker sans bananas

sipped her share of first-class bubbly, and didn't have a clue as to how (or why) one would balance a checkbook.

Remarkably, however, the sometimes self-indulgent star blazed with fervor for numerous causes less *célèbre* than her own amusement. An intrepid and enthusiastic intelligence-gatherer for the French Resistance, she received the highest military honors offered by her adopted country after World War II. Back in the U.S. in the 1950s and '60s, she became a tireless crusader for civil rights, marching with Martin Luther King, Jr., refusing to perform in any venue from which blacks were routinely barred, and playing a large part in integrating American night clubs and theaters. And the heartbreaking yet inspiring story of her "rainbow tribe"—the twelve children of various races and religions that she adopted, planning to raise them in a public "showplace for brotherhood"— deserves a cinematic treatment of its own.

"If I'm going to be a success, I must be scandalous," Baker once observed. Seldom has that particular show-biz strategy been so succinctly stated, or so aptly demonstrated. One of the great overachievers of all time, Baker managed to lead a life that was successfully scandalous, scandalously successful—and also a rare credit to the human race.

"I must amuse."

—JB

Headstrong Hedy

When the earth moved for Hedy Lamarr (then known as plain old Hedwig Kiesler) in the 1933 Czech film *Ecstasy*, it also rocked the rest of the movie-going globe. In a now-famous shot seen 'round the world, the bodacious Austrian bit player, no more than nineteen at the time, seemed to reach the peaks of, well, *ecstasy*—while skinny-dipping in a lake. (Must have been something in the water.) On-screen nudity being a universal no-no at the time, *Ecstasy* was banned in Germany, denounced by the Pope, and eagerly screened by anyone who could get his hands on a print.

In the end, that turned out to be a lot of anyones—including Lamarr's future mentor, MGM starmaker Louis B. Mayer—despite the desperate efforts of Fritz Mandl, her hubby, to buy up and burn all evidence of his wife's orgasmic plunge. And yes, just as you might suspect, the Mandl marriage (number one in Lamarr's series of six) simply wasn't destined to last. Fascist Fritz, a wealthy munitions magnate, was obviously quite the control freak. Moreover, the Mrs. never did take a shine to his business associates—Mussolini, Lamarr would later say, struck her as "pompous," while Hitler was always "posturing."

But Hollywood, U.S.A., where Lamarr immigrated in 1938 (she disguised herself as a servant to escape her spouse and his scary Nazi cronies), was initially thrilled to host her. In the professional opinion of Mr. Mayer, a man who certainly knew from cheesecake, his dishy new discovery was simply "the most beautiful creature on earth." He promptly provided her with a suitably mellifluous new name (hasta la vista, Hedwig) and, over the next decade or so, numerous opportunities to exhibit her lovely looks to appreciative American audiences.

"When she spoke, one did not listen," rhapsodized George Sanders, Lamarr's co-star in the 1949 film *Samson and Delilah*. "One just watched her mouth moving and marveled at the exquisite shapes made by her lips." As it turned out, however, the leading lady's acting abilities weren't quite as exquisite as the motions of her mouth. Although *Samson and Delilah* certainly turned a respectable profit, Lamarr starred in numerous other films of the '40s without, as cinema chronicler Ephraim Katz put it, "creating a pandemonium at the box office."

Perhaps, however, the directors who invariably cast Lamarr as a woman of mystery sensed that she had more on her mind than keeping her lines (and/or the names of her numerous lovers) straight. And indeed, we now know, the "most beautiful woman in the world" was also, thanks to the tutoring of ex-spouse Fritz, the Fascist munitions man, something of a whiz in the field of military materials design. Although her concept of a radio-controlled torpedo never did come to fruition, in 1942 Lamarr (with composer friend George Antheil) secretly patented a remote-controlled radio system that allowed signals to be transmitted without being detected or deciphered.

To Lamarr's great regret, the U.S. military made no use of her "secret communication system" until the 1960s (she had hoped it would help defeat the Nazis). Meanwhile, her Hollywood career had fizzled, and her name appeared on the news only when she was picked up on the occasional shoplifting charge. But the former bathing beauty wasn't *quite* washed up in the fame and fortune department. Recently, it seems, a brand-new generation of cellular phones and wireless modems has sprung from the still-smoldering ashes of her decades-old invention. And in 1997, the once-notorious nudist (now an eighty-four-year-old Florida recluse) finally received a lifetime achievement award— from the Electronic Frontier Foundation.

"Any girl can be glamorous. All you have to do is stand still and look stupid."

—*HL*

Lovely Lamarr was a closet nerd

HERE'S LOOKING AT YOU, KID

From daring to downright dangerous, the beauty secrets that make the stars look different from you and me...

Marilyn Monroe wasn't born with a wriggle in her walk—she strategically removed a smidgen of a shoe heel to give herself a suggestively swaying gait.

"I owe a lot of my performance to the corset I had to wear....
The blood rushes to your face when you wear
those things. So that explains 'radiant.'"
—**Emma Thompson, accounting for her glowing reviews
(and complexion) in *Howards End***

Joan Crawford extracted her back teeth toward the end of more diva-esque cheekbones.

"I'll use science to help nature if that's what I feel like."
—**Brigitte Nielsen**

"The thing that separates us from the animals is
our ability to accessorize."
—**Olympia Dukakis (in *Steel Magnolias*)**

According to some, film star/fitness queen Jane Fonda acquired that willowy wisp of a waist by yanking a rib or two. (Talk about going for the burn!)

"I have no regrets. Regret only makes wrinkles."
—**Sophia Loren**

A self-described "purist," Kirstie Alley swears by her anti-aging oxygen machine. Each and every day, Alley takes nozzle in hand and spritzes her facial pores with youth-enhancing molecules for half an hour. "Oxygen revives the dead in hospitals," notes the well-aerated actress, "so what do you think it does if you breathe it all day?"

"You can wear red with red hair," maintains Molly Ringwald. "They say you can't, but you can, and I do—and I look good." As we all know, modest Molly also looks pretty in pink.

Cool Catherine Deneuve had two words for a reporter wondering about the source of her so-called "ageless beauty": "I breathe."

★ ★ ★

And then, of course, there are those low-maintenance types who happen to think they look A-O.K. au naturelle, thank you very much...

At the age of forty-five, the former Lancôme model and *Blue Velvet* sensation Isabella Rosselini boldly posed for *Allure* magazine sans so much as a smidgen of makup...a state that would scare the living highlights out of any middle-aged woman who hadn't inherited Ingrid Bergman's genes (or her balls).

"This whole plastic surgery thing as moral dilemma makes me
nauseous. It's a question of, do I mutilate myself for the
sake of people making money off me or not?"
—Martha Plimpton

Cheeky comedian Tracey Ullman is quite, quite certain that she didn't use a body double for her nude scene in *Ready to Wear*. "With that big cellulite ass rolling across the screen, it had to be me," she explains. "I don't know where you'd find buttocks like mine, dear."

"I feel more naked with makeup on than I do without it."
—**Brooke Shields**

Just for the hell of it, actress Ann Magnuson once gave herself a beauty "make-under" (bad false teeth, bottle-thick glasses, mismatched roots) before venturing into a few of Manhattan's tonier emporiums. It does the soul good to get in touch with the "Inner Hag," she concluded, but few entrepreneurs are eager for the I.H. to try on the Tiffany bracelet or the spring collection from Chanel.

"The most beautiful female star in filmdom is Lassie. She transcends all boundaries; she's a totally gorgeous sincere actress and at once a bitch and man's best friend. With gorgeous hair, yet."
—**Patsy Kelly**

"I'll look at a photo of a movie star from the '30s, all made up and glamorous, and I'll wonder if she had her period that day. Or did she have to go out with some guy from the mob that night?"
—**Tracey Ullman**

Grace Notes

Grace Kelly's career got off to a royally slow start. Though the Philadelphia millionaire's daughter had the three Bs down pat (she was blonde, beautiful, and bred very, very well) the only parts she could land were in T.V. cigarette commercials. Needless to say, it would never do for a Princess to be seen pushing Marlboros. So it was certainly fortunate that the former cigarette girl had become a glitzy glamour girl—and even won an Oscar for *The Country Girl* in 1954—by the time she met Prince Ranier III the following year. With great fanfare, the man from Monaco would soon sweep her off to live happily ever after (and, more importantly, bear him heirs) in his kingdom by the sea.

Selling smokes, however, was small potatoes compared to another pre-nuptial matter that might have nipped Kelly's triumph in the bud. Guys who sit on thrones, as you may have noted, tend to get even more ticked-off than your average Joe when they suspect hanky-panky on the part of a mate. And we'd rather not dwell on all the royal wives who have been summarily divorced or decapitated for not being as chaste as they'd once suggested.

Well, apparently unbeknownst to Rainier, Hollywood scuttlebutt had it that his fiancee wasn't quite as frosty as she looked in her films. Yes, the young lady with the virginal visage, seldom spotted without her dainty white gloves, was known around town as the "Snow Princess" long before she became a *real* Princess. But Alfred Hitchcock, who directed the cool ingenue in three films, including *Rear Window* (1954), coined the nickname with purely sarcastic intent. "Grace almost always laid the leading man," author/dirt-disher Gore Vidal (a Hollywood scriptwriter in Kelly's day) would later prattle. "She was notorious for that in this town."

Gary Cooper, Clark Gable, Bing Crosby, William Holden, the very married Ray Milland...all are said to have fallen into Kelly's not-so-chill clutches en route to a wrap. Throw in Oleg Cassini (the designer who did Jackie Kennedy up in style), the playboy Prince Aly Khan, Frank Sinatra on the rebound from Ava Gardner, and scads of other alleged boyfriends du jour, and you can see why many perceived the "Snow Princess" as something of a one-woman heat wave. "She wore those white gloves," one insider would later recall, "but she was no saint."

Kelly, for her part, turned the coldest of shoulders to those scandalized by her exploits. "Hollywood amuses me," she scoffed. "Holier-than-thou for the public and unholier-than-the-devil in reality." And we all know who got the last laugh: a certified M.D. swore to Rainier that Kelly was fully fit (so to speak) to be his spouse, and Monaco's main man made the promiscuous actress a Princess with no apparent qualms. (Also, it was rumored, he needed the hefty dowry her daddy provided to keep his casino afloat.)

Princess Grace of Monaco perished, of course, in a car crash in 1982, under circumstances that remain cloudy to this day. Long before her death, however, she fulfilled her end of the matrimonial bargain by producing little Caroline, Albert, and Stephanie. And if even one-tenth of what you read in the tabloids can be construed as true, Grace's now-grown progeny have certainly done their best to carry on in Mama's regal but racy tradition.

"We live in a terrible world. A man kisses your hand and it's screamed out from all the headlines. He can't even tell you he loves you without the whole world knowing about it."

—GK

A princess with a past

It's the Money, Honey

Sarah Bernhardt, she has never claimed to be. But who, dahling, would have *wanted* to follow in Bernhardt's footsteps—*beaucoup de beaux* but only one husband, and no nice jewelry to speak of? Certainly not Zsa Zsa Gabor, the ageless European charmer celebrated for her many monied spouses (eight in all, a Turkish diplomat, a German nobleman, and the man who invented Barbie among them)—plus a stockpile of gemstones big enough to float the national debt.

Let's face it, few have ever considered Gabor, the original high-maintenance babe, a major feminist icon—except, that is, for the glamour girl herself. "Who the hell wants any handouts from a man? I like to earn my own way," insists the convent-educated beauty, crowned Miss Hungary 1936 at the age of—but never mind about that! Precisely *how* Gabor has traditionally brought home the bacon, however, isn't your typical Susan B. Anthony story. (No, she didn't land in the top tax bracket simply for adorning *Lovely to Look At*, *Lili*, and a handful of other films of the '50s and '60s.)

"Zsa Zsa knew more days on which gifts can be given than appear on any holiday calendar," sighed Conrad Hilton, the magnate who co-starred in Gabor's second marriage (to this day, his ex gets a 25 percent discount when she stays at any Hilton hotel). "The most expensive courtesan since Madame de Pompadour," groused one U.S. congressman. And from the clothes-horse's very own mouth: "Rubi [international playboy Porfirio Rubirosa] loved me so much he bought me the whole Christian Dior collection every season."

Still, no one ever went bankrupt on Gabor's behalf, since the burden of keeping her in baubles has been shared by so many suitors over the years—J. Paul Getty, Lord Mountbatten, the Duke of Marlborough, Prince Phillip, John F. Kennedy, Henry

*The Gabor gals get down
(from left: Zsa Zsa, Eva, Magda)*

Kissinger, George Sanders, Richard Burton, Sean Connery, Frank Sinatra, Charlie Chaplin, and Nicky Hilton (her own stepson), to name only a few of the generous guys with whom Gabor has been either loosely or tightly linked. ("Their husbands and their dalliances have made a loose-leaf address book a necessity," noted one friend of Gabor and her equally socially-active sister, Eva.)

Having acquired so much expertise in the field, Gabor shared some personally-patented tips in *Zsa Zsa's Complete Guide to Men* (1969) and *How to Get A Man, How to Keep a Man, and How to Get Rid of a Man* (1971). One male whom she failed to finesse, however, was the Beverly Hills traffic cop who pulled her over in 1989 (something tedious, it seems, about the Rolls' expired plates). The former beauty queen (also a princess, countess, and duchess by dint of marriage) slapped the officer silly—and spent three days in the slammer as a result. But so what if a grand old gal's tiara slips from time to time? In Gabor's case, you can bet, there are plenty more where it came from.

> *"Dahling, any intelligent woman can find her target and she can marry him."*
> —ZZG

GABOR TALKS

"I believe in large families; every woman should
have at least three husbands."

"I am a marvelous housekeeper. Every time I leave
a man, I keep his house."

"I only wear my diamonds just to aggravate my friends."

"Husbands are like fires. They go out when unattended."

"I could never be in love with an Italian. They are not even faithful
when they are faithful."

"I had affairs. But dahling, it's not like I slept with all
those men in ten days."

"Maybe I meet Mr. Right tomorrow."

A Wet Dream Come True

L et's put it this way: nobody ever showed up at an Esther Williams flick expecting to see her play Lady Macbeth. "I can't sing, I can't dance, I can't act," the world-class athlete who morphed into "Hollywood's Mermaid" once observed—and no, she wasn't just being modest.

Of course, Williams (a physically-fit nymphette of nineteen when she showed up—and how!—on the set of *Andy Hardy's Double Life* in 1942) never actually aspired to be the next Joan C. or Bette D. A super-talented teen swim champion, she set a record in the 100-meter-breast stroke in 1939 and snared a spot on the U.S. Olympic team. But World War II wiped out any possibility of the scheduled Summer Games in Helsinki proceeding as planned, and Williams became a part-time I Magnin model instead of an Olympic medalist.

Fearful of making a fool of herself, Williams turned down the first MGM scout who offered her a contract, and accepted the second only on the condition that the studio set her up with six months of acting lessons. But she needn't have worried: the escapist pool-side musicals that would make her famous seldom called for Williams to do much more than show off her sensational choreographed strokes, look super while smiling under-water, and plant the occasional big wet one on her male co-star. Compared to declaim-ing Shakespeare, Williams found water-ballet a piece of cake, and her popularity soared. Between 1944 and 1955, she appeared on more fan magazine covers than any other female star, and by 1949 ranked second only to Betty Grable as a box office draw.

Under the circumstances, it's not surprising that the so-called "Queen of the Surf" acquired a little (okay, a lot of) attitude along the way. The story goes that she once flashed her bare breasts at a fan who gushed—once too often—that his friends would

Williams flexes her P.R. muscle

never believe he had met her. "The guy said nobody would believe him," she snickered. "I made sure that nobody would." And when fellow actor Fernando Lamas popped the question—complete with that sweet old-fashioned line about wanting to take her "away from all this"—Williams wondered if she had water in her ears. "Away from all what?" she icily inquired. "I'm a movie star!"

Not until the fad for frou-frou extravaganzas with titles like *Bathing Beauty* and *Neptune's Daughter* started to fade in the late 1950s did Williams' acting career finally bottom out. "Wet she's a star, dry she ain't," one producer said. As far as we can tell, the one-time Olympic hopeful, who wound up hawking backyard pools and bathing costumes, would have been the first to agree.

"My pictures are put together out of scraps they find in the producer's wastebasket."
—EW

"I'm a ballbuster, blonde or brunette!"
—Ashley Judd

GOING, GOING, GONE

What price fame? Someplace between $287.50 and $20,700, recent research reveals. Following, a smattering of sums that certain Hollywood artifacts once fetched on the auction block...

A bed shared by Clark Gable and Carole Lombard (and God knows who else):	$20,700
A bed shared by Britt Ekland (and God knows who else):	$658.48
Marilyn Monroe's high school yearbook:	$3,450
Mae West's makeup case:	$1,840
Joan Crawford's makeup case:	$747.50
Part of one of Julie Andrews' costumes from *The Sound of Music*:	$29,900
Jayne Mansfield's compact:	$345
Ginger Rogers' compact:	$287.50
Barbra Streisand's vanity (no comment!):	$3,220

6

Defiant Divas

Prissy Fights Back

"Lawdy, Miz Scarlett, I don't know nuthin' 'bout birthin' babies!" Think of Butterfly McQueen, and you think of her *Gone with the Wind* performance as Prissy, the hysterical housemaid who didn't know quite as much about mid-wifery as she liked to let on. In fact, there was nothing even slightly flighty about the former dancer (and former Thelma) who took her stage name after performing "The Butterfly Ballet" in a production of *A Midsummer Night's Dream*. A self-possessed woman of twenty-eight when she debuted as the dimwitted Prissy in 1939, about all McQueen shared with her laughably addle-pated character was her sex and her race. Nonetheless, she was forced to fight the Prissy imprint for the remainder of her Hollywood career.

McQueen emerged as a force to be reckoned with on the set of *Gone with the Wind*, when she refused to shoot a scene that showed her eating watermelon. The assertive actress didn't win a campaign to stop Scarlett from slapping Prissy when she confesses to not being an OB/GYN after all, but it was known to all that she found the scene demeaning. But while her one-woman war against racism couldn't have made McQueen very popular with (or on) the Scarlett O'Hara set, it didn't save her from the scorn of Malcolm X, who once wrote that he was both ashamed of and angered by her role.

"I didn't mind playing a maid the first time because I thought that was how you got into the business," McQueen would later tell an interviewer. But silly, servile Prissy parts were all that came her way during the '40s (*Mildred Pierce, Affectionately Yours, Duel in the Sun*), and "after I did the same thing over and over I resented it." Eventually, McQueen started passing on parts that portrayed black women in cliché roles—not that there was a surfeit of any other kind. And by 1947, Hollywood (where casting agents often refused to work on her behalf) had obviously had it with the uppity actress as well. Unwilling to compromise her principles, McQueen spent the next twenty-five years doing subsistence-level jobs instead of dazzling movie-goers. At the age of sixty-four, she earned a Bachelor of Arts degree from City College of New York, and was hired as a Harlem schoolteacher.

Not every black actress of the era would have considered McQueen's life a success—her Oscar-winning *Gone with the Wind* colleague Hattie McDaniel, for example, deliberately chose a less confrontational, more upwardly-mobile course. But for the perennial Prissy, it was preferable to perform menial jobs in real life than to play maids in movies.

"I didn't mind being funny, but I didn't like being stupid."
—BM

LOTUS BLOSSOM SAYS SHOVE IT

Much in demand during the Jazz Age fad for Asian mystery movies, Chinese-American actress Anna May Wong wearied of playing stereotyped parts. When Caucasian Luise Ranier nabbed the meaty, supposedly-Asian female lead in *The Good Earth* (1935), Wong made her point by turning down the (same ol', same ol') dragon lady role that was thoughtlessly tossed her way instead.

In Livid Color

Being nobody's fool, the young Lena Horne didn't waste her time hoping that Hollywood would discover her. For one thing, by the age of sixteen, most of that time was already occupied supporting her family—first on her chorus girl's salary at Harlem's Cotton Club in 1933, then as a Broadway chorine, and finally as a nationally known nightclub singer. A member of the NAACP since the age of two (an activist grandmother signed her up), and a black American since birth, Horne also couldn't help but think long and hard when all-white Hollywood beckoned in the early 1940s.

In fact, the first black performer ever to sign a long-term Hollywood contract may also have been the most reluctant individual ever to do so. Only when friends convinced Horne that black Americans would be inspired by seeing her on-screen did she make her barrier-smashing deal with MGM in 1942. Justifiably paranoid about being typecast as a Mammy or a maid, she demanded—and received—a guarantee that she would not have to play stereotyped parts.

Once MGM had signed Horne, however, it didn't seem to know quite what to do with an entertainer who, as she herself noted, "looked exactly like everybody else in Hollywood, except I was bronze." Sometimes, she was allowed to shine in an extraneous musical guest spot that was excised from the version of the film that Southern audiences saw. On other occasions, she was rejected for a part because her skin color was too *light*. (According to one story, Max Factor invented "Little Egyptian" makeup specifically to help Horne remedy this particular "problem.") And the only speaking part for which MGM found her suitable for was in the all-black film *Cabin in the Sky* (though she landed another in Fox's all-black *Stormy Weather*.)

Horne fought racism in full makeup

A maverick in her private as well as her professional life, Horne braved the wrath of a nation (and a mailbox brimming with hate mail) when she married white musician Leonard Hayton in 1947. When a drunk Beverly Hills restaurant patron hurled the epithet "nigger" her way, she hurled an ashtray, a lamp, and several drinking glasses right back. And during the madness of the McCarthy years, she remained true-blue to blacklisted friends in the entertainment industry—at the price of being blacklisted herself.

Today, we applaud Horne—still vibrant and vital in her eighties—as an all-around show business phenomenon rather than a movie star. (Her 1981 one-woman show, *Lena Horne: The Lady and Her Music*, became the longest-running production of that genre in Broadway history.) But even though Hollywood proved the validity of her most pessimistic expectations, "the sepia Hedy Lamarr" (as Horne wryly called herself) did succeed in depicting a more sophisticated and glamorous image of black womanhood than American moviegoers had previously seen. "The image that I chose to give them," she observed pointedly, "was of a woman who they could not reach."

"It was a damn fight everywhere I was, every place I worked."
—LH

The Silent Star of the 1950s

I n 1950, Judy Holliday took home an Oscar for her performance as a brainless blond in *Born Yesterday*. Wet behind the ears, however, the curvy comic actress (then in her late twenties) was not. According to a widely-circulated story, Holliday fended off one ill-bred producer's pass by whipping off her falsies and flinging them in his face. "Here's what you're after," she smirked.

Some versions of the anecdote have Darryl F. Zanuck of Twentieth Century-Fox as the badly-behaved boy, while others attribute the hands-on behavior to Columbia Pictures' Harry Cohn. Whoever the cad in question, however, Holliday was simply more woman (with or without her falsies) than old-school movie moguls knew how to handle.

Blessed with a sky-high I.Q. and a comedic gift that critics compared to Charlie Chaplin's, the native New Yorker debuted in what one critic termed a "moronic" Broadway role in 1945, and caused a sensation as the ditzy Billie Dawn in *Born Yesterday* the following year. By the time Harry Cohn got around to casting the celluloid version of the drama, Holliday had reprised her signature role 1,600 times on stage, and played a similar scatter-brained part in MGM's *Adam's Rib*.

Nonetheless, Cohn hated the idea of hiring the casting couch hold-out, who also refused to sign a contract requiring her to make more than one picture per year. Then there was the fact that Holliday, like Cohn, was a Jew. "Films are made for Jews and by Jews—not *with Jews*," he insisted. But the would-be movie star held her ground, and after an exhaustive two-year, *Gone with the Wind*-style search for the definitive Billie Dawn, Cohn finally conceded that Holliday should have the role. (Graciousness, however, still eluded him: "I guess I worked with fat asses before!" he snickered, contemplating her un-Hollywoodesque heft.)

In the end, of course, every last one of Cohn's fears proved unfounded, and Holliday beat out both Bette Davis in *All About Eve* and Gloria Swanson in *Sunset Boulevard* for the Best Actress award. But fans of America's zaniest new screen queen (who succumbed to cancer in her early forties) never did get to see her finest performance. That tour de force took place before the House Un-American Activities Committee, though fortunately the pinko-persecutors never knew it. Subpoenaed to testify about her supposedly treasonous activities and acquaintances, Holliday turned in such a convincing performance as a dumb blonde that the Committee couldn't get a sensible answer out of her, let alone the name of a single Communist sympathizer.

"I started as a moron . . . and I worked up to be an imbecile in Adam's Rib.
What I want to know is: where does a girl go from being an imbecile?
Maybe, if I'm lucky, I can be an idiot or a cretin."
—JH

IT DIDN'T PLAY IN BEIJING

She didn't play a stripper, or star in an arty low-budget film. But for twenty-seven-year-old Chinese actress Bai Ling, simply accepting a role as Richard Gere's attorney in the 1997 film *Red Corner* was a heavy-duty risk. Beijing bureaucrats were so freaked by the politically-pointed film, in fact, that Bai Ling deemed it safer to stay in Hollywood than return to her homeland. On a brighter note, she was subsequently cast as Jon Bon Jovi's sweetie in *Row Your Boat* (and while we're on the subject of subversive, let's give a nod to Mr. Bon Jovi's powerful effect on youthful female hormones).

DEEPER THAN SHE LOOKED

These days, it's usually considered alluring if a woman happens to have the kind of speaking voice that suggests something along the lines of a two-pack-a-day smoking habit. Back in 1943, however, the unusually deep timbre of her utterances almost sent June Allyson to the sidelines during her first small film role in the MGM musical *Best Foot Forward*. The first day she showed up on the set, in fact, the husky-voiced neophyte (cast as a teen-prom-goer) was ordered to go home and stay there

The tenor-next-door type

until her health improved. "I haven't got a cold," protested Allyson. "I talk like this all the time." And so, as the perennially perky (and permanently low-pitched) actress went on to demonstrate in over thirty films—*Best Foot Forward* among them—she did.

THE LONGEST INTERMISSION

Stuart in her salad days

Who said there are no second acts in American life? Well, F. Scott Fitzgerald did—but in the case of long-lived leading lady Gloria Stuart, he happened to be dead wrong. Over half a century after retiring from the silver screen (she was sick of parts that seemed "dreary and stupid"), at age eighty-seven-year-old Stuart suddenly resurfaced in an major role in the 1997 epic, *Titanic*. (For what it's worth, Stuart also made a splash in the 1937 film *Girl Overboard*.) The oldest performer ever to be nominated for an Academy Award, Stuart was regularly slathered with tons of makeup on the set: otherwise, she simply looked too young for her part.

The Mystery That Is Christie

*T*alk about a tease! A mesmerizing Age of Aquarius screen queen, Julie Christie eluded Omar Sharif in *Dr. Zhivago*, tantalized real-life beau Warren Beatty in *Shampoo* and *Heaven Can Wait*, and walked away with an Oscar for her performance in *Darling*. Then, when aficionados of the ethereal yet engaging beauty were every bit as hooked as her co-stars, Christie decided the limelight just wasn't her thing. "I'd rather talk to my ducks than some of the freaks I met in Hollywood," she said, and only seldom in the past two decades has a director coaxed her away from her farm in Wales.

Actually, Christie's fling with Hollywood fame was touch and go from the start. The India-born daughter of a British tea planter, she initially avoided an acting career because—oh, *please*—she considered her features homely. Nor was her relocation to Los Angeles in the 1960s a carefully-calculated career move. "I was there because of a lot of American boyfriends," the erstwhile wild child later revealed. And in the end, Christie pursued a career as a movie star, she claimed, only because "I've no qualifications to be anything else." (Hmmm . . . guess they don't teach typing in those toney British boarding schools.)

Who knew that the actress Pauline Kael once dubbed "the sexiest woman in movies" would wind up in rubber boots and overalls, mucking about in the manure a million miles from the site of her youthful triumphs? And while Christie has scraped the mud from her soles long enough to appear in a handful of movies since the 1980s, her post-Hollywood passions suggest the earth mother more than the sex goddess. A rabid environmentalist, she campaigns against nuclear power, for animal rights, and prides herself on having no central heating in her ancient stone farmhouse—pelts from her fleecy flocks provide warmth the natural way. (Very *Far From The Madding Crowd*, no?)

In fact, it turns out, Christie is such a dyed-in-the-wool do-your-own-thing type that she has never even tried to submit to the bonds of matrimony. "Some people can be married and some people cannot—it's as simple as that," she has said. This doesn't mean, however, that the self-aware spinster relies exclusively on those sheepskins to keep her warm at night—for close to two decades now, investigative journalist Duncan Campbell has been the lucky man in Christie's life.

If you're one of countless fans still carrying a torch, or if circumstances caused you to miss out on the first wave of Christie-mania (perhaps, for example, you hadn't yet been born), do try to catch her rare performance in the 1998 film *Afterglow*. Lured from her crunchy-granola causes to star in the love story, fifty-six-year-old Christie is said to be "incandescent" as ever in her latest role. Not, of course, that this down-to-earth diva is even slightly interested in contemplating her eternal mystique. "I'm not a myth or a legend," she insists, "just somebody who works in films."

"Marriage—it's like signing your life away."
—JC

THE CALL-BACK OF THE WILD

Lions and tigers never have fazed Tippi Hedren, the cool blonde cast by horror-meister Alfred Hitchcock in the 1963 thriller, *The Birds*. In fact, headstrong Hedren (known for spurning Hitchcock's advances and spawning Melanie Griffith) is said to roll out the red carpet for feral felines of every stripe. The king (and queen) of beasts once roamed her California ranch at will, and instead of a cuddly kitty-cat, a live pet leopard lolled on little Melanie's bed. Research does not reveal, however, how Hedren feels about our feathered friends.

A woman of primal passions

WOMEN OF ACTION

Some actresses set the world on fire. Others get their kicks from going up in flames themselves—or plunging from pinnacles, or leaping from speeding cars. No, you don't have to be bonkers to pull seemingly suicidal stunts for a living. But, we gather, it helps....

And you thought *your* daily grind was grueling! "I look forward to going to work and going through a window," adrenalin addict Jennifer Watson once gushed. "To me, it's like diving into a swimming pool." Watson, who performed her favorite pane-ful maneuver in *Back to the Future III* (1990), has wisely selected a paramedic as her beau.

Silent film actress Mabel Normand is said to have tried her hand at the occasional stunt. Of course, Normand is also said to have ingested superhuman quantities of drugs.

Maria Kelly has taken the fall for Teri Hatcher, Gwyneth Paltrow, and Meg Ryan during the course of her own high-impact career. She has also survived eighteen concussions, which may or may not explain why $10,000 once made it worth her while to Jet-Ski over a waterfall.

A former Malaysian beauty queen, Michelle Yeoh is the rare actress who doesn't use a double for the dangerous stuff. In her first American film,

Tomorrow Never Dies (1997), the bantam-weight Bond girl showed off some of the moves that make her Hong Kong's highest-paid leading lady. Not all of them, though: concerned about insurance coverage, MGM put the kibosh on any completely kamikaze maneuvers. "I have dislocated my shoulder," Yeoh boasts. "I've cracked my share of ribs. I've ruptured an artery. But I have never broken a bone."

Leading lady Dorothy Lamour looked great lounging by the sea in her sarong. Steel-nerved Lila Shanley, who performed Lamour's fancier underwater feats, made sure that the glamour girl kept her powder (and her sarong) dry.

LaFaye Baker, one of Hollywood's few black stuntwomen, is listed in the *Guinness Book of World Records*. Not, however, for her heart-stopping LaFaye flambé routine (we've seen the pictures, and trust us, they're terrifying), but for the teenage feat of setting fifty-eight hula hoops in simultaneous motion.

Daredevils who don't like pain would do well to pass themselves off as men. As Linda Howard, former president of the Stuntwomen's Association of Motion Pictures, once noted: "I've never seen a stuntman working who wasn't in black Reeboks, but women get thrown down stairs in a negligee and high heels. No room for kneepads there."

NOW HEAR THIS

In 1986, hearing-impaired actress Marlee Matlin took home an Oscar for her screen debut as a fiercely independent deaf woman in *Children of A Lesser God*. (As you may recall, she also took home co-star William Hurt, her significant other at the time.) Far from mellowed by her moment of fame, this precedent-setting celebrity now crusades for deaf rights in non-theatrical arenas, and absolutely refuses to be interviewed on T.V. programs that are not close-captioned.

"I wasn't afraid for my safety. I'd rather take a bullet in the head than not make a movie."
—Lara Flynn Boyle, on the subject of shooting
***The Big Squeeze* (1996) in Los Angeles gang territory**

Leapin' Lizards

A Broadway actress lauded for her 1929 performance in *Tommy*, Peg Entwistle gambled that she'd hit the fame-and-fortune jackpot in Hollywood. The transition from stage to screen proved rocky, however, and though enterprising Entwistle hustled for months, all she landed was a bit part in *Thirteen Women*.

Even at the end of her emotional rope, however, Entwistle didn't lose her creative flair. Carbon monoxide, of course, was a cliché. Sleeping pills had been done to death. And any girl could slash her wrists. But no other washed-up actress had ever thought to leap, as Entwistle did in 1932, from the lofty Hollywood Sign—then actually the "Hollywoodland" Sign—overlooking the City of Broken Dreams.

Ironically, "Hollywoodland" itself represented another colossal failure: it was the hilltop site of a real estate development that never quite panned out for Keystone director Mack Sennett. And speaking of irony...right around the time of Entwistle's Big Pitch, the Beverly Hills Community Players was deciding to toss her a meaty tailor-made part in its next production—as a gal who does herself in.

It's too bad that Entwistle wasn't around to appreciate all this irony, of course. On the other hand, her fifty-foot plunge proved an unanticipated smash success in the Major Downer genre, briefly transforming the obscure actress into the topic du jour, and spawning a lemming-like wave of fellow leapers who found her feat a devastatingly...well, *ironic* way of signing off.

BESIDES, IDOL WORSHIP IS A SIN

Elvis Presley was the King. But God ranked even higher with Dolores Hart, who starred with the swivel-hipped heart-throb in two films of the '50s (*Loving You, King Creole*). Shortly thereafter, devout Dolores retreated into a Roman Catholic convent, and was never seen on the screen again. The now-sexagenarian Sister did make a few worldly waves in 1998, however, when she announced that, contrary to one old hound-dog of a rumor, she had never, ever been preggers with Presley's love-child.

7

Scarlet Sirens

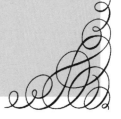

Olive's Twist

A budding starlet still in her teens, Olive Thomas wasn't the kind of girl that movie mogul Myron Selznick was compelled to chase around the casting couch. "So this is where I get laid?" snickered Thomas (or so the story goes) as she sauntered into his infamous lair. And when she finally emerged, coveted contract in hand, she was Selznick Pictures' hottest new silent star.

Needless to say, it would have been nice if Ms. Thomas had been encouraged to prove her mettle in a less horizontal fashion. (Also, it would be nice if human beings were unfailingly kind to one another, and when it rained, bouquets of pretty posies fell out of the sky.) On the other hand, you have to hand it to this gal for making the most of some rather meager raw material. Born into an impoverished Pennsylvania mining family around the turn of the century, she posed for pornographic photos at ten, became a wife at twelve, and ran away to Harlem at fourteen (she even had to steal her bus fare).

Things started to look up, however, when Thomas (who was *almost* as good-looking as she was gutsy) won a newspaper beauty contest for "The Perfect Model." Soon her fresh young face was gracing the pages of *Vogue* and *Vanity Fair*, and in 1915, she won a starring role in the Ziegfeld Follies. One of the first "Vargas girls," she posed unclothed for the Peruvian cheesecake portraitist, and was termed "the most beautiful woman in the world" by artist Harrison Fisher.

Her colorful *curricula vitae* and a secret drug habit notwithstanding, Thomas still managed to look (and act) like the proverbial choirgirl in popular Hollywood comedies of the late Teens like *Betty Takes a Hand, The Follies Girl,* and *Prudence on Broadway.* Cast from day one in wholesome "kid sister" roles, she even signed off on a series of articles advising American girls to remain pure in thought, word, and deed. And to top off the whole facade, the much-ballyhooed model of maidenhood wound up marrying actor Jack Pickford, brother to golden girl Mary—and the so-called "Ideal American Boy."

Needless to say, then, it came as quite a shock to the public when, in 1920, twenty-year-old Thomas suddenly turned up dead, disrobed, and chock-full of bichloride of mercury capsules in a toney Paris hotel. More than one fan must have choked on her bubblegum when investigators revealed that the clean-living screen idol had spent the final hours before her suicide boozing it up, palling around with French gangsters, and possibly trying to score some heroin. And no less a film buff than the Cardinal of Chicago was so bummed to learn about Miss Goody Two Shoes' evil alter ego that he sat right down and scribbled a tract titled *The Danger of Hollywood: A Warning to Young Girls*. Somehow, though, it doesn't seem that the Cardinal's cautionary opus was very widely read...

> *"I smoked a lot of dope. I made it with a lot of guys. I tried every way*
> *I could think of to act just as bad and outrageous as I could."*
> —Actress Elizabeth Ashley (born in 1939)

Saturday Night Fervor

Praise Alla! Hollywood sybarites of the '20s invoked the holy name day and night. No, a vogue for Islam didn't suddenly sweep the Colony. The risqué soirees hosted by racy Russian immigrant Alla Nazimova, however, *were* all the rage—as was the smoldering silent film star herself. Seances, orgies, stars frolicking sans their frocks—anything went when naughty Nazimova got into the hostess groove at the "Garden of Allah," her lavish three-acre estate on Sunset Boulevard. And guests in search of more sedate shenanigans could always retreat to Mary's, a lesbian bar on Sunset Strip that top-grossing Nazimova *also* owned.

Not, you understand, that Nazimova popped from the womb in full decadent flower. Born in Crimea in 1879, the hardworking hedonist debuted as a professional violinist and acted under Stanislavsky (well, under his direction, anyway) before emigrating to America in 1905. Dark, intense, and a gifted interpreter of Ibsen, she electrified the Broadway stage and even established her own New York theater before venturing into the celluloid realm.

As libidinous Left Coast types soon discovered, however, Nazimova had plenty of passion left for a rather Hugh Hefner-esque social life. At one typically titillating "Garden of Allah" affair, twenty naked starlets leapt into the pool (built in the shape of the Baltic Sea), while quasi B-girl Barbara La Marr posted a sign reading "Come One, Come All" on a nearby bungalow, and proceeded to make good on the offer. It's not quite true, however, that the ultra-bohemian hostess had *no* house rules: guests were required to address Nazimova as "Madame," and for reasons of superstition, no one was ever allowed to say "good night."

Biographers disagree as to whether enigmatic Nazimova (billed, appropriately

Alla works the Gothic angle

enough, as "The Woman of a Thousand Moods") and her colleague Charles Bryant ever tied the knot—and if not, then exactly *why* not. But according to most accounts, fabulous females were forever dropping at her exotic Russian tootsies—including both of Rudolph Valentino's wives, one of Charlie Chaplin's, and a niece of Oscar Wilde. In fact, Nazimova is often credited with coining the phrase "sewing circle" to describe a simpatico clique of lesbians in the arts.

From the much-romanced vamp's fertile imagination also sprang an all-gay production of *Salome* in tribute to Oscar Wilde. (The famously flaming author was so taken by the head-severing Old Testament tale that he based an 1895 stageplay on it.) Well, outré Oscar would probably have loved Nazimova's highly stylized 1923 spectacle featuring hordes of homosexual actors, a script by her lover Natasha Rambova, and the sultry star/producer herself performing the Strip-Tease of the Seven Veils.

The critics, however, were not charmed, the film was a commercial disaster, and "The Woman of a Thousand Moods" returned (probably in a very bad one) to stalking the stage. She died in 1945, leaving behind "The Garden of Allah," which flourished as one of Hollywood's most notorious hotels for a number of years—and god-daughter Nancy Reagan, who flourished as one of America's most notorious first ladies.

"Somebody should write a book, All About Alla, *or something. . . .
she's more interesting than almost any actress
from the sound era."*
—Producer Irene Mayer Selznick

SHE SUCKED, SHE REALLY SUCKED

In 1896, thirty-four-year-old stage comedienne May Irwin became the first actress ever to pucker up for a brief on-screen lip-lock. The instantly-notorious film was called *The Kiss*, and Ms. Irwin was called immoral by various members of the clergy who somehow found it necessary (or not!) to view the smooching scene in question. Chicago publisher Herbert S. Stone, on the other hand, took offense on aesthetic grounds. Neither Irwin nor her co-star, he complained, were the least bit "physically attractive," and "the spectacle of their prolonged pasturing on each other's lips was hard to bear."

A show biz veteran since the age of thirteen, Irwin (characterized by one biographer, just in case you were wondering, as "a plump, jolly blonde") probably did not take her peculiar critics—and aren't they all?—to heart. It is unlikely, also, that the bound-for-hell busser sought prolonged spiritual counseling, or sat around waiting for someone to hurry up and invent liposuction. For whatever reason, however, Irwin did not attempt a second film role for another eighteen years.

Brava Brooks

"I like to drink and f***," silent star Louise Brooks often proclaimed—and so, it seemed, she did. A former Ziegfeld Follies girl nicknamed "Hellcat" by her cohorts, Brooks partied heartily and bedded as many lovers as she pleased (and not necessarily one at a time). According to film critic Ken Tynan, she was not only "the most sexual image of Woman ever committed to celluloid," but "the only pure pleasure-seeker I have ever known." Yet oddly enough, this amorous expert couldn't plant a kiss on a posterior to save her own life—or, more to the point, her career.

Boyishly bobbed (if you ask us, Vidal Sassoon owes this lady big-time) and barely clad, twenty-year-old Brooks piqued the prurient interest of Jazz Age audiences in *The American Venus* (1926), a *very* revealing look at the Miss America pageant. And when it came out that Brooks had once posed nude for a New York photographer, her erotic image was further enhanced, even though she supposedly didn't intend the pictures to be pornographic. "I pictured myself in the Louvre trying to imitate various works of the old masters," the high-minded model later explained.

Brooks went on to make several more successful Hollywood films with Paramount. Word was, however, that she took a rather whimsical attitude toward the work ethic. For reasons that may have involved her alleged unreliability as much as her supposed unsuitability for talking parts, the studio proposed a significant salary cut in the late 1920s. The peeved starlet made a rude counter-proposal, and the curtain fell on Phase I of her career.

Weeks later, Brooks was kicking up her heels in decadence-drenched Berlin, where, she later wrote, "sex was the business of the town." But it wasn't just the recreational opportunities that had Brooks bubbling. One of 1,600 actresses (among them Marlene Dietrich) tested for the 1929 classic *Pandora's Box,* the sultry American had nailed the

Bad girl Brooks on a good hair day

nymphomaniac role on which her artistic reputation largely rests. (As for the *other* kind of reputation—well, let's just say that Brooks did her fair share of homework before concluding that "the best lovers I ever had were homosexuals.")

Paramount didn't get any fonder of Brooks during her European exploits, and the feeling (or lack of it) was mutual. Just to spite the studio, she refused to reshoot her silent movies in sound. And just because she didn't want to, she also refused to loll on the casting couch at Columbia Pictures, or so the story goes. Eventually, Brooks took up nightclub dancing to keep herself in liquor and lounging gowns, got herself arrested for "lewd cohabitation" in Kansas, and wound up as a saleswoman at Saks Fifth Avenue in New York.

Long before her death in 1985, however, the forgotten femme fatale enjoyed a renewed surge of public interest in her work, thanks to the efforts of James Card, the curator of the Kodak International Museum of Photography. According to some, Mr. Card also saw fit to jump-start his idol's libido, but their scandalous affair (an irate wife was part of the picture) foundered when Brooks repeatedly drank him under the table.

If you're interested in hearing similarly salacious stories straight from the horse's mouth, Brooks' memoir *Lulu in Hollywood* belongs at your bedside. Needless to say, babbling Brooks was not the type to go quietly into the good night, and sharing her still-heated feelings about the film industry, plus a great deal of interesting information about her sex life, must have been a "pure pleasure" indeed.

> *"The nastiest gal I've ever seen. It was known all over how bad she was."*
> —Ethylene Clair, a cinematic colleague of Brooks

MAD A(BOU)T YOU

Love means never having to say *what*? Whether passion sizzled—or whether it fizzled—apologizing for their brazen behavior never even occurred to the following Hollywood honeys. . . .

Fans of Ingrid Bergman, the hitherto wholesome dentist's wife who starred in *Casablanca,* were shocked when she turned up extra-maritally pregnant in 1949. But so what? "Even if the whole world should fall on me, I don't care," declared the defiant adulteress, whose fetus was fathered by director Roberto Rossellini. "This is my child and I want it." In the end, of course, the scandal cost Bergman more than her good name: the U.S. Senate denounced the Academy Award-winning Swede as a "free love cultist" and "a powerful influence for evil," and she was blacklisted from American films for seven years. Which was, by the way, approximately the same length of time that Bergman's belated marriage to Mr. Rossellini—which produced two tiny twins in addition to the original bastard—lasted before it was annulled.

"I'm not upset about my divorce," quipped abundant T.V. and movie talent Roseanne when she split from tattooed hubby Tom Arnold. "I'm only upset I'm not a widow."

One of Sharon Stone's assorted former flames, Hart Bochner, took to calling her "The Antichrist" after his ardor had cooled. Stone, for her part, once let it slip that she deemed another ex, Dwight Yoakam, the equivalent of a "dirt sandwich." Well, you can't change human nature—but trust a

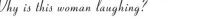
Why is this woman laughing?

power player like Stone to turn it to her advantage. After swiping producer Bill MacDonald from his wife, but before consenting to cohabit, the star made besotted Bill swear that after the inevitable split, he was legally forbidden to trash her. Now, here's the beauty part: according to their non-nuptial contract, Stone was free to shoot off her mouth about him.

"I never believed marriage was a lasting institution," Lauren Bacall once mused. "I thought that to be married for five years was to be married forever." Yet only death could part her from Bogie—and it did, twelve years after she said "I do."

No wonder she nabbed eligible-bachelor-no-longer Nicholas Cage on the first try. What red-blooded man _could_ resist a till-death-do-us-part proposal from the vampy (or vampirish) Patricia Arquette, all dolled up in black vinyl and toting a virulent purple wedding cake?

★ ★ ★

In a perfect world, ha, we'd all meet Mr. or Ms. Right the second we were finally ready to commit. Classy Hollywood gals, however, at least try to come up with a gracious exit line when giving the boot to a boo-boo beau. For example, as Nicollette Sheridan said to Harry Hamlin: "You're boring, stupid, and I don't have any fun with you. Good-bye."

Marie McDonald, a curvy starlet of the 1940s, couldn't help it if she was known for her seven marriages instead of her many mediocre films. "Husbands are easier to find than good agents," shrugged the beauty often dubbed "The Body."

Like any smitten suitor, William Randolph Hearst made up pet names for his mistress Marion Davies—the movie star's clitoris, for example, was known to the couple as "Rosebud." It's a further testament to Davies' intestinal fortitude that she didn't ditch the newspaper nabob the second she got wind of the Orson Welles masterpiece known as *Citizen Kane*.

Davies: No shrinking violet

Not only did that 1941 classic make her out to be a boob, but obviously somebody had spilled the beans about the couple's cutesy-poo pillow talk. What, you thought Welles named the red sled "Rosebud" at random?

★ ★ ★

And on the subject of fragile flowers..." Lovers are like roses—best by the dozen," proclaimed Barbara La Marr in the 1920s. An overdose of narcotics, not a surfeit of sex, killed the exquisite silent star.

Funny Valentinos

What do women want? Well, in the '20s, *one* thing they wanted was Rudolph Valentino—a dark, broodingly sensual ladies' man much given to gold jewelry, chinchilla-lined coats, and the use of women's cologne. For half a decade, this luxuriously-groomed dandy *ruled* as the cinema's numero uno male sex symbol (and never mind that his resume included a stint as a taxi dancer and several arrests for petty theft). At the premiere of *The Sheik* in 1921, women fainted in the aisles en masse. And Valentino's sudden death at thirty-one (more likely the result, some whispered, of a miffed mistress than his perforated ulcer) provoked some of the most flamboyant displays of grief ever witnessed by Hollywood gossip reporters.

Unlike thousands of others who sobbed over Valentino's coffin in 1926, however, his ex-wife Jean Acker didn't lament the loss of the world's greatest lover. In fact, the aspiring actress never even got a taste of her husband's supposedly oft-sampled wares. Acker—generally acknowledged to have been a lesbian—locked Valentino out of the bridal suite on their wedding night, and the marriage collapsed before it was ever consummated.

No, we don't know what inspired this very temporary Mrs. Valentino (a lover of Alla Nazimova, then Hollywood's most sought-after sapphite) to tie the knot in the first place—or to unravel it six hours later. "He thought more of making love to the camera than to me," she "explained" to one syndicated columnist, but obviously there was a little more—or a little less—to the story than that. Eventually, however, Acker summoned up sufficient wifely feeling to sue Valentino for spousal support. And even after the pair divorced, she continued to use "Mrs. Rudolph Valentino" as her stage name—a practice that provoked set designer Natasha Rambova, the *second* Mrs. Rudolph Valentino, into a lawsuit-filing rage. (Presumably, it also swelled Acker's box office booty a bit.)

Go figure. Like Acker, Rambova (whose made-up Russian moniker was quite an improvement over her *previous* name, Winifred Shaunessy Hudnut) was also a lover of the womanizing Ms. Nazimova. Like Acker, she too failed to make wifely nooky with America's Most Wanted Male. (Rambova's nickname, incidentally, was "The Icicle.") For whatever reason, however, Valentino was in such a hurry to hook up with his second non-hetero honey that he didn't *quite* manage to get himself divorced from the first, and briefly wound up in the slammer on bigamy charges. And to top it all off, the guy was so crazy about Wife No. Two that he agreed to wear a gold "slave bracelet" symbolizing his total submission to her.

In time-honored husbandly tradition, Valentino referred to his second spouse as "The Boss." Chez Valentino, however, the term was anything but a joke. Guided, she believed, by supernatural powers, Valentino's butch better half not only ruled the roost at home, but also micro-managed her hubby's career. Script selection, casting decisions, costuming, set design—Rambova (or her powers) held passionate opinions on such topics. Meekly, the star who sported a slave bracelet did as he was told…until studio executives became so incensed by the Mrs.'s helpful "hints" that her on-set presence was specifically forbidden in Valentino's movie contracts.

In retrospect, it's clear that Rambova wasn't blessed with superlative commercial instincts. She "allowed" her husband to make *The Sheik* against her better judgment—and the film went on to break all box office records. And under her guidance, Valentino's screen image grew increasingly effeminate, so much so that one widely-circulated Chicago *Tribune* editorial labelled him a "painted pansy," a "pink powder puff," and an overall threat to the American way of life. Nor did it boost his status with the testosterone sector when Rambova revealed, after the pair finally parted ways, that the Great

Lover had failed (or perhaps not even tried) to bed either one of his wives.

Neither insinuations of homosexuality nor death itself, however, stilled the savage passions that the silent era's Sex King aroused in the female heart. Mobs of hysterical mourners thronged the New York funeral parlor where his body lay in state, and not even a thousand of the NYPD's finest were capable of keeping the ladies in order. In London, an actress who had never even met Valentino committed suicide while gazing at his inscribed photo (and in Paris, an elevator boy did the same). A New York woman hitchhiked across the country to keep vigil over Valentino's Hollywood tomb, and couldn't be coaxed away by her husband for several days.

And for decades after his death, a mysterious "Lady in Black" was spotted (and sometimes photographed) strewing roses over Valentino's marble crypt on the anniversary of his demise. Somehow, though, we doubt that the fetching veils of this femme flame-keeper concealed either one of Rudolph Valentino's remarkably virile wives.

"I can play a heterosexual. I know how they walk. I know how they talk.
You don't have to be one to play one."
—Lily Tomlin

ABOUT BEING OUT

A high-voltage honey

"Vibrators," born-again lesbian Anne Heche once mused. "I think they are great. They keep you out of stupid sex." Speaking of which, many wondered whether hitherto-straight Heche had lost her marbles (or, perhaps, her batteries) when she trumpeted her passion for sitcom Sappho Ellen DeGeneres to the world in 1997. But Heche (who has since starred in the romantic comedy *6 Days, 7 Nights*) isn't worried about sabotaging her hetero leading lady career. "They should ask me if I can play gay!" she recently noted. "I've had very little practice being gay."

WELL-KNOWN ACTRESSES WHO HAVE PLAYED BISEXUALS OR LESBIANS IN FILMS— AND LIVED TO TELL THE TALE

June Allyson	*They Only Kill Their Masters*
Elizabeth Ashley	*Windows*
Lauren Bacall	*Young Man With a Horn*
Candice Bergen	*The Group*
Claire Bloom	*The Haunting*
Dyan Cannon	*Doctors' Wives*
Cher	*Silkwood*
Catherine Deneuve	*The Hunger*
Greta Garbo	*Queen Christina*
Whoopi Goldberg	*The Color Purple*
Mariel Hemingway	*Personal Best*
Shirley MacLaine	*The Children's Hour*
Melina Mercouri	*Once is Not Enough*
Bette Midler	*The Rose*
Barbara Stanwyck	*Walk on the Wild Side*
Meryl Streep	*Kramer vs. Kramer*
Liv Ullman	*Persona*
Shelley Winters	*The Balcony*

*Adapted from *Lesbian Lists* by Dell Richards.

Hurricane Lupe

According to some, Lupe Velez was just another convent girl gone wrong. Others claim she veered from the righteous path when Mama Velez, a Mexico City streetwalker, started selling her teenage daughter's favors. In any event, temperamental Velez—the so-called "Mexican Spitfire" of the '20s and '30s—seems to have done her best to live up to both the racy rumors and her racist nickname. (Somehow, Hollywood has never pegged anyone as a "Scandinavian Spitfire"—or, for that matter, a "Mexican Cold Fish.")

Velez got her first big break at eighteen, when she starred opposite Douglas Fairbanks in *The Gaucho*. From there, it was just a hop, skip, and a jumping bean to becoming *the* tempestuous leading lady of the day. The fiery star of features like *Lady of the Pavements* and *The Squaw Man*, Velez was typecast as a live wire even in the *Mexican Spitfire* comedy series she made toward the close of her career.

Velez didn't have many mellow off-screen moments, either. Her dramatic, traumatic, and high-decibel love/hate life was the talk of the tabloids, and a big boon to gossip columnist Hedda Hopper, Velez' across-the-street neighbor. Her passionate 1929 affair with Gary Cooper, according to one biographer, left the male movie star "exhausted," and sometimes black and blue as well. It also nearly left him in the morgue—in a fit of pique, Velez once fired a gun at him through the window of a slow-moving train. (According to her ultra-creative P.R. flacks, she *had* to shatter the window so she could give her sweetie a smooch.)

Velez' violent feelings for Tarzan (aka Johnny Weissmuller, to whom she was briefly wed) posed quite a challenge for the MGM make-up crew: it seems that the King of the Jungle often showed up for his bare-chested shoots covered with love-bites and claw

Velez: The picture of drop-dead glamour

marks. (The combustible couple also made sure that the busboys at Ciro's earned their wages the night they toppled a food-laden table in the course of a conjugal spat.)

"The first time you buy a house you think how pretty it is and sign the check," Velez once said. "The second time you look to see if the basement has termites. It's the same with men." But as time went on, she grew more lax in her inspections, and in the giant footsteps of Tarzan followed a string of low-life lovers approximately as long as the Rio Grande.

"There has never been another like her—so stormy, so merry, so warmhearted," claimed Velez' friend, the writer Adela Rogers St. Johns. But like a summer hurricane, volatile Velez was just passing through. The year was 1944, and the thirty-six-year-old star was expecting a child with sometime-beau Harald Ramond, who seems to have enjoyed the act of conception far more than the concept of playing Papa. At the time, unwed motherhood wasn't quite the chic celebrity avocation it is today. Nor did Velez care for the concept of an illegal abortion (perhaps she really *was* a convent girl after all).

Under the circumstances, the only line that readily came to mind was "Adios." But as you might imagine, Ms. Velez did not intend to go unnoticed into that good night. She ordered dozens of flowers, transforming her boudoir into a perfumed shrine. She consulted her hair stylist. She sat for a session with her cosmetician. She decided on a fetching silver lamé gown. And only when she was completely ready for her close-up did Velez chug a bottle of Seconal, and take her place in the pantheon of Hollywood's highly dramatic suicides.

"I make love when I'm in love."
—LV

Talullah's Lulus

"**I** want to try everything once," claimed Tallulah Bankhead. Or was that *everyone*? Brazen Bankhead was, of course, probably the most audacious actress America (well, an awful lot of it, anyway) has ever known. Well-known for spreading her own perverse brand of P.R., the bisexual sybarite once boasted that her lovers numbered someplace in the vicinity of 5,000. Hence her oft-quoted quip: "I'm as pure as the driven slush."

Contrary to the impression she cultivated, however, Bankhead didn't start life as a full-blown scarlet woman. Born in 1902 into a distinguished Alabama family (Dad was speaker of the House of Representatives, Grandpa was well-known Senator John Hollis Bankhead), the boldest Bankhead ever to walk the face of the earth was—believe it or not—educated in a convent.

You'd never guess it, though, from the subsequent bad behavior of this shameless Southern belle. Propelled into the limelight when she won a beauty contest at age fifteen, Bankhead became the toast of the London stage in her twenties—not to mention becoming *toasted* (or tipsy, or pixilated, or just plain high) as often as she could. "My father warned me about men and booze," she purred, "but he never mentioned a *word* about women and cocaine."

As you might expect, Bankhead's rapier wit and raspy baritone went over big with London's more liberated and/or lesbian ladies, and critics did not fail to observe that her most ardent fans were female. On the other hand, the switch-hitting Yank didn't altogether ignore the gents—though she did often embarrass them. "Darling, you're as good as the King of England," she once bellowed out the window after a departing lover. And when a former beau (accompanied by his new sweetie) pretended not to notice her, she gave as good as she got. "What's the matter, darling?" she inquired. "Don't you recognize me with my clothes on?"

Bankhead's proclivity for outrageous extracurricular activities never vanished—in fact, the final word she ever spoke was "bourbon." Nonetheless, the hard-living hedonist (who returned to the United States in 1930) went on to garner a New York Film Critics award for her performance in Alfred Hitchcock's *Lifeboat,* turn in stellar performances in several stage plays of the 1940s (most notably, *The Little Foxes* and *The Skin of Our Teeth*), and come within a corseted inch of snagging the coveted Scarlett O'Hara role in *Gone with the Wind*.

Speaking of man-eating minxes (or minks): The great mating maven Alfred Kinsey, agog at the thought of the thousands who traipsed through Bankhead's boudoir, once begged her to tell him all about her sex life. "Of course, darling," she deadpanned, "if you will tell me about yours." Somehow, we doubt that the reserved researcher ever got an earful about all the women (or, for that matter, the men) that Bankhead is said to have wooed—among them the unlikely trio of Joan Crawford, Hattie McDaniel (the Academy Award-winning "Mammy" of *Gone with the Wind*), and eccentric evangelist Aimee Semple McPherson.

Critical assessment of Bankhead's professional stature varies today—some consider her to have been a "brilliant" artist; others, an attractive but untrained actress whose talents were moderate at best. Few would dispute, however, that this fascinating figure gave an over-the-top performance in her real-life role as a libertine, a lecher, and an utterly devastating wit. As Alfred Hitchcock so succinctly put it: "The whole point about Tallulah was that she had no inhibitions."

"Nobody can be exactly like me. Sometimes even I have trouble doing it."
—TB

Tallulah liked to show a little leg, etc.

FLAMBOYANT FLASHERS

Can over-exposure really ruin a rising star's career? True, that very personal glimpse of glamour girl Sharon Stone in *Basic Instinct* incited a certain amount of puritanical controversy in the land of the free, home of the depraved. (To which there was at least a modicum of Darwinian logic—had those madcap Mayflowerites spent even twenty seconds of a New England winter in a skivvy-less state, severe frostbite would have been the result— and where, in the most literal sense, would we be then?) Yet despite her sin of omission, sexy Stone (who, according to gossip guru Liz Smith, sports pricey La Perla underpinnings in real life) continues to land leading lady roles to this day. What's more, research reveals, "let it all hang out" was the philosophy of many a daring dyed-in-the-wool diva (including Jean Harlow and Carmen Miranda) decades before our Miss Stone, born in 1958, made her maiden appearance as a bare-bottomed babe...

Certainly the colleagues of Lupe Velez could be forgiven for muffing their lines. Velez was notorious for lolling about film sets of the 1930s and '40s sans her lingerie.

Typecast as a perennial gangster, George Raft temporarily lost his tough-guy bravado when he happened to witness Carole Lombard applying peroxide in the bikini zone. "Relax, Georgie," Lombard giggled. "I'm just making my collar and cuffs match."

According to actor Donald Sutherland (that's Kiefer's dad to you whippersnappers), he found it impossible not to stare when an utterly unclad Tallulah Bankhead sauntered into his dressing room. "What's the matter, darling? Haven't you ever seen a blonde before?" teased the exquisite exhibitionist.

★ ★ ★

And let us not, by the way, rush to label the distinguished Mr. Sutherland as a hopeless lech. Judging by the record, it was the rare Hollywoodite who *didn't* get an unsolicited gander at Bankhead's genitalia in her heyday. On one notable occasion, she emerged from co-star Joan Crawford's dressing room in a stark-naked state—except for the conspicuous sprinkling of gold glitter in her pubic hair. (Crawford, by the way, was known for highlighting the hair on her *head* with glitter.) "Guess what I've been doing?" bragged (or lied) Bankhead.

GREAT EXPECTATIONS

Demi Moore proved just how provocative pregnancy can be when she posed nude—and near term—on the cover of *Vanity Fair* in 1991. Two years later, Demi's own madcap mama struck a blow against grandmotherly stereotypes by doffing *her* duds for a so-called "men's magazine." The unclad (and essentially estranged) crusaders did not, however, rekindle the '50s fad for matching mother-daughter outfits.

HOLLYWOOD SQUARES

Trashy Tallulah Bankhead boasted of bedding 5,000 lovers. Starlet Barbara La Marr's corps of sex partners is likewise said to have numbered in the thousands. And as the purpler pages of Hollywood history suggest, such pre-AIDS profligacy wasn't precisely an anomaly. Yet according to our own carefully-compiled virile statistics, some of the world's biggest fans of matrimony have also managed to make out pretty well in Sodom-by-the-Sea...

ACTRESS	NUMBER OF HUSBANDS
Constance Bennett	5 husbands
Joan Crawford	5 husbands
Arlene Dahl	6 husbands
Zsa Zsa Gabor	8 husbands
Judy Garland	5 husbands
Rita Hayworth	5 husbands
Hedy Lamarr	6 husbands
Marie McDonald	7 husbands
Jane Powell	5 husbands
Martha Raye	7 husbands
Ginger Rogers	5 husbands
Gloria Swanson	6 husbands
Elizabeth Taylor	7 husbands (and 8 weddings)

Lana Turner	7 husbands
Mamie Van Doren	5 husbands
Total Actresses: 15	Total Husbands: 89

IT'S A GIRL!

Even as a pre-schooler, future Oscar-winner/unwed mother Jodie Foster wasn't your average little girl. In fact, the tough-as-nails tyke who started hawking sunscreen at the age of three wasn't *any* kind of little girl—or so she claimed when she auditioned for her first Coppertone commercial in 1965. "I told them that my name was Alexander," the precocious gender-bender would later recall. "I kept showing them how I could make muscles." A quarter of a century later, Foster cleared up any residual confusion on the subject of her sex when she showed up at the Academy Awards in unbuttoned Armani—and not in a blouse or a bra.

Something to Think About

It was no accident that Gloria Grahame, chronically cast as a fallen angel during the '50s, exuded come-hither vibes that were practically palpable. "To look sexy you've got to be thinking sexy while you're playing the scene," explained the analytical temptress. "It wasn't the way I looked at a man, it was the thought behind it." Grahame thought so hard that in 1952 she won an Academy Award as Best Supporting Actress for *The Bad and the Beautiful* (she, of course, was both).

Grahame spent lots of time exercising her mind in real life, too. Four times a bride in her fifty-six years, she selected as her final spouse a gent some fifteen years her junior, and the son of husband #2, to boot! According to one story, in fact, the little guy was barely old enough to shave when his sultry stepmother first lured him to her bed.

But love à la Woody and Soon Yi didn't play any better in the '60s than it does now. "From the press's reaction—and some of the public's, too—you'd have thought I was committing incest or robbing the cradle," the steamed scene-maker later marveled. "*All my marriages have been ordinary.*" And so they were—at least the way that Grahame thought.

8

Off-Screen Schemers

The Guy Who Invented the Movies

*A*t first, Alice Guy's prospective boss wasn't sure if she was even qualified to be a secretary. Sure, she could type (a more unusual skill in 1895 than it is today), but Leon Gaumont, owner of a Parisian photography studio, worried that she was a touch too youthful for the job. "I'll get over that," the then-twenty-ish Guy reassured him—and the position (for what it was worth) was all hers.

Quite the quick study, Guy soon got an idea or two of her own about the motion picture camera that Gaumont, along with a handful of other European and American innovators, was in the process of pioneering. Though the new technology was initially considered a tool for documenting real-life occasions, Guy saw that it presented artier possibilities. She also saw that Gaumont didn't mind if she experimented with his equipment (provided, of course, that she continued to crank out her quota of Gal Friday tasks). The result, in August 1896, was the world's first fictional film, the one-and-one-half-minute *La Fée au choux* (*The Cabbage Fairy*)—entirely written, directed, and produced by the twenty-three-year-old secretary.

No, Guy's fanciful mini-pic (based on a fairy tale about children born in the midst of smelly veggies) didn't zap her forthwith to the realm of the rich and famous. It did, however, liberate her from her day job. The big boss, it seems, liked his helper's handiwork so much that he immediately set up the now-legendary Gaumont Studios for her—and gave her carte blanche to do what she wanted. (Which did not, as you may imagine, include much typing or filing.) During the ensuing decade, Guy would make almost four hundred films for Gaumont, trying her hand at myriad then-experimental techniques, among them the use of color, sound, and the special effects necessary to raise Jesus from the dead in her 1906 epic, *The Life of Christ*.

The cute cabbage patch kids scenario aside, Guy didn't do a lot of what we now term "chick flicks"—unless you count *In the Year 2000*, a fantasy film (needless to say) about a world ruled by women. What she *did* do: adventures, science fiction, novel adaptations, comedy, horror, and even one vampire picture. Nor, it should be noted, did her status as a member of the gentle sex seem to inhibit her from depicting the violent crashes, collisions, and explosions that movie-goers then, as now, found so strangely compelling.

In 1907, Gaumont's girl genius finally took her talent (and her no-good husband, Herbert Blaché) to Fort Lee, New Jersey, where she formed her own production company, Solax. The first woman ever to own and run her own film studio, Guy spent another ten years at the helm of her state-of-the-art enterprise, writing, directing, and producing another 300 films.

Who knows what would have happened if Guy had continued to make movies for the rest of her life. Maybe women really *would* rule the world—or at least the silver screen. But in the early 1920s, a major domestic disaster, coupled with fierce competition from the male-run money machine known as Hollywood (where, by the way, Mssr. Blaché had recently absconded with his mistress), effectively terminated Guy's hitherto stunning career. She returned sans spouse to France, her two small children in tow, and quickly faded into obscurity. Fortunately, however, this extraordinarily prolific film pioneer also proved extraordinarily long-lived, so she was at least able to savor the moment when, in 1953, the French government finally got around to naming the then-eighty-year-old Guy to the Legion of Honor for her enduring contribution to the art of film.

> *"Only in hindsight does [Guy] qualify as a woman who broke the mold;*
> *she worked when there was no mold to break."*
> —Glenn Kenny

A Highly Dramatic Affair

*M*ove over, Suzanne Sugarbaker! Long before the boob tube was even invented, Aline Bernstein, the *original* designing woman, was exerting her boffo influence behind the scenes…that she so brilliantly conceived. Born in 1880, native New Yorker Bernstein (like many another artsy turn-of-the-century type) studied to be a portrait painter. Thanks to her work as a volunteer for a local playhouse, however, her career took a few unexpected turns, and by the 1920s, Bernstein was rising to prominence as America's first female theater designer of note.

The artistic spirit behind the spectacular sets of the Hollywood extravaganzas *She* and *The Last Days of Pompeii*, Bernstein also collaborated on several productions of Lillian Hellman's plays, co-founded the Costume Institute of the Metropolitan Museum of Art, and designed scores of innovative stage sets during her wide-ranging theatrical career.

Married, and the mother of two, she also found time (though not until her late forties) to squeeze in a sizzling five-year affair with Thomas Wolfe. At the time, few had ever heard of the now-acclaimed novelist, then a struggling scriptwriter some twenty years Bernstein's junior. (In other words, about the age of her own offspring.) Nor did love blind Bernstein to her himbo's lack of talent—as a playwright, that is. Due to her candid comments, the young dramatist abandoned his awkward attempts to write for the stage, and tried his hand at a rather well-received first novel: *Look Homeward, Angel.*

Unlike Wolfe, his influential mentor never did become a household name, though Bernstein continued to design stunning sets and win rave reviews for her work (not to mention a prestigious award for opera costume design) into her seventies. She did, however, become the fictional "Esther Jack" in Wolfe's *The Web and the Rock* and *You Can't Go Home*

Again—a fittingly artistic tribute to the creative dynamo who launched not one, but *two* dramatically successful careers.

"I want no fences around me, unless I erect them myself."
—Faye Dunaway

THAT'S COLD

Hollywood just wasn't happening for Nell Shipman, a very independent filmmaker who flourished in the early '20s. An ardent, ahead-of-her-times environmentalist, Shipman insisted on outdoor locations, challenging-to-hazardous shooting conditions, and utterly unfrivolous themes. She also insisted on setting up her production company in isolated Priest Lake, Idaho—far, far, from the madding crowd.

Many of Shipman's films featured wild animals, and she was a pioneer in promoting their humane treatment on the set. Not until the 1930s, in fact, did the Society for the Prevention of Cruelty to Animals begin to enforce similar standards. It must have slipped Shipman's mind, however, that human beings are also animals: the male lead in *Back to God's Country* (her commercially successful first film) perished of pneumonia while shooting scenes in the chilly wilderness of Alberta, Canada.

Moviemaker With a Mission

_T_he highest-paid director in silent films, and the first American-born woman in the profession, Lois Weber directed over a hundred pictures between 1912 and her death in 1939. Not, you understand, that directing was a lifelong ambition—the cinema didn't even exist when Weber was born in 1882. Nor was it by any means her first career: Weber trained as a concert pianist, served as a Salvation Army street evangelist, toured with her husband's theatrical company, and acted in a few screen productions herself before finding her professional niche at Universal Studios. In 1916, this multi-talented pioneer (who also wrote and starred in many of her films) even gave politics a go, and was elected mayor of Universal City.

Throughout her life, Weber found film an ideal medium for exploring hot-button social issues. _Hypocrites_ (1914), featuring actress Margaret Edwards in the cinema's first clothing-optional love scene, created quite a stir. So, in a different sense, did _Where Are My Children_ (1916), a candid exploration of the subject of birth control. By 1920, Weber's work had attracted the attention of Paramount Studios, which offered her $50,000 a picture, plus one-third of the profits. To the now-seasoned director's irritation, Paramount publicity made much of her supposedly unique perspective as a woman—but hey, the money was good.

At the height of her popularity, Weber's work was as well-known as that of D.W. Griffith or Cecil B. De Mille, and she made far-ranging plans to experiment with the use of film in education. As time went on, however, audiences began to find the former proselytizer's films a touch too preachy, and her final productions (including one talkie in

1934) received poor reviews. Weber died in 1939, a major influence in the field of socially relevant films.

"People have been modeling their lives after films for years, but the medium is somehow unsuited to moral lessons, cautionary tales, or polemics of any kind."

—Renata Adler

A BRIEF ENCOUNTER

The first time Barbara Boyle visited the Charlie Chaplin Studio, she didn't get the part. That was okay with Boyle, though, since she wasn't really interested in portraying a bikini-clad bombshell. In fact, the recent law school grad wasn't interested in acting at all—as far as she knew, she was interviewing for a position in the studio's legal department, not a role in the beach party film then being cast.

The year being 1960, however, personnel automatically routed the young woman to a producer's office—where, much to her surprise, she was promptly ordered to disrobe. Only after delivering "a long diatribe about women, images, and what Hollywood generated about both" did it dawn on Boyle that she might be in the wrong place. Her chutzpah, however, so impressed the producer that he recommended that the legal department hire her on the spot, and Boyle (today an independent movie producer) went home as an employed lawyer instead of a starlet, which suited her—so to speak—just fine.

BALLS OF STEEL, ET AL.

In 1987, Dawn Steel was named president of Columbia Pictures, making her the most powerful female executive ever in the film business. "I don't feel there's a glass ceiling," the former college dropout (who succumbed to cancer in 1997) once said. "If I had felt it, I wouldn't have gotten to where I got."

Terminator 2 co-producer B.J. Rack had no time for leading lady/hard-bodied mommy Linda Hamilton's complaints about juggling motherhood and movies. Fact was, Rack didn't even have time for her own mini-brood of two. "Five and six," she guess-timated when questioned about her children's ages. Actually, they were eight and nine. But hey, *Terminator 2* was a totally rad flick!

A supremely successful Hollywood agent, the now-retired Sue Mengers began her career as secretary at William Morris. The ambitious go-getter gained many a client with her confrontational cry, "Your career sucks!"

"There is no downside to success," claims Sherry Lansing. We'll take her word for it: Lansing has served as chairman of Paramount's Motion Picture Group since 1992,

Too Direct for Her Own Good

"The greater part of the motion picture audience is feminine," director Dorothy Arzner noted in 1936, the year she helped found the Directors Guild of America. "If there are no women directors, there ought to be." Yet another hidden-from-history Hollywood heroine, Arzner directed Paramount's first talkie, invented the boom microphone, transformed the genre of women's films—and, for many years, occupied the only female director's chair in Hollywood.

A medical school dropout, a World War I ambulance driver, and, many writers hint, a blatant butch, the "mannish" Arzner arrived at Paramount shortly after the end of the war with the definite intention of becoming a director. But though she quickly rose through the pink collar ranks—typist, script reader, editor, chief editor, scenario writer—her repeated requests to do more were essentially treated as bad jokes. Finally, one Paramount executive's wife intervened on her behalf, and in 1927, Arzner was assigned to direct a film called *Fashions For Women* (guess why?).

The picture was a success—and Arzner was forever consigned to the realm of women's films. "They would avoid me for westerns or action pictures," noted Arzner, who had previously written and edited *The Covered Wagon*—the world's first famous western. "If it was a love story, then they thought of me."

Fortunately, Arzner's studio-prescribed specialty was one which not only interested her, but for which she had a real flair. She went on to direct Clara Bow in the smash hit (and prototypical female buddy movie) *The Wild Party*, help forge Katharine Hepburn's powerful and androgynous image in her second movie, *Christopher Strong*, and transform Rosalind Russell into a star in *Craig's Wife*. Of her seventeen films, however, *Dance Girl Dance* (1940) is today considered Arzner's finest; according to film historian Kevin Jack Hagopian, it was crucial in sparking "the renaissance of interest" in women's filmmaking in the 1970s.

Directors were not celebrities in Arzner's day, she once observed; they more closely resembled "hired help." Yet Arzner insisted on autonomy, and one of her Columbia contracts even noted that she was not required to attend meetings aboard Harry Cohn's yacht. "To be a director you cannot be subject to anyone, even the head of the studio," she once told a reporter. "I threatened to quit each time I didn't get my way, but no one ever let me walk out."

All that changed in 1943, however, when Arzner suddenly left the set of Columbia's *First Comes Courage*, just one week short of a wrap. Though the studio cited her ill health, there was clearly more to the story, and Arzner never directed another Hollywood picture. To the day she died, she maintained a stony silence surrounding the subject of her abrupt departure. But fellow director (and fellow alleged gay) George Cukor spoke for many when he voiced his theory. A devotee of cropped hair and men's attire, Arzner "didn't modify her ways or looks or manner," he once observed. "As a woman directing movies, she was looked on by most as a freak. And as *that* kind of woman, they found her less and less acceptable."

Cross-dressed and cosmetic-free, Arzner went on to direct WAC training shorts, a venue in which a buzz cut was presumably not entirely out of place. She also made fifty or so Pepsi-Cola commercials featuring her close friend (and, some say, lover) Joan Crawford, and launched filmmaking programs at U.C.L.A. and the Pasadena Playhouse. She died in 1979, having had the satisfaction of seeing her work rescued from the metaphorical cutting room floor to which so many women's accomplishments have been relegated.

> *"I wasn't prepared to stay in pictures if I had to cave in to demands*
> *and interference which I felt were unfair."*
>
> —DA

Arzner models her power suit

The Baddest Writer in the West

Premise: Far-out female screenwriter, a charter member of Hollywood old girls' network, makes like Robin Hood with studio funds, saves down-and-out actress's career....

Well, *we* happen to love the "Thelma (and/or) Louise Does Hollywood" theme—and so, we gather, did Frances Marion, the prolific, powerful, and fiercely feminist scribe who actually performed the above feats. The highest-paid screenwriter in Hollywood from 1916 to the mid-1930s, Marion authored 150 original stories and adaptations during the course of her career...and those were just the ones for which she got credit.

Plenty of women wrote for the movies in Marion's day, among them well-known Anita *"Gentlemen Prefer Blondes"* Loos, and Adele Buffington, the author of over 150 rough-and-tumble westerns. According to Library of Congress statistics, in fact, fully half of all films made prior to 1925 featured the work of women authors. Marion, too, had a gift for great scripts (*The Big House, The Champ, Stella Dallas, Anna Christie, Dinner at Eight,* and *Camille* are just a few of her well-known works), but it was her profound faith in woman-to-woman networking that makes her a recently rediscovered feminist icon.

Termed "the pillar of my career" by Mary Pickford, Marion penned many of the silent star's pictures, and was her closest friend as well. Lillian Gish, Marion Davies, and Marie Dressler were likewise long-term cronies/collaborators. And when Marion and Pickford teamed up for the first time on the Famous Players film *The Poor Little Rich Girl* in 1917, director Clarence Brown would later recall, "spontaneous combustion" was the result. But surprise, surprise—male movie execs weren't crazy about the unprecedented estrogen explosion, and informed the pair that their maiden effort was almost too "putrid" to release. Later, the two women would surreptitiously sneak into the jam-packed theaters where the film was playing, savor the audience's delight, and swear never again to listen to a group of guys.

"Women . . . reach out to others like plants to the sun," Marion once wrote, "but men at work get swept into the vortex." Neither unaware of nor embarrassed by her classically feminine way of working, she reveled in the role of team player—as long, of course, as the team wasn't the kind with testosterone. In 1930, she carefully constructed the MGM film *Min and Bill* as a comeback vehicle for her friend Marie Dressler, an actress who had fallen into such disfavor that she was practically destitute. Not only did *Min and Bill* win Dressler an Academy Award, but it also allowed the scheming screenwriter to help another woman in need, the writer Lorna Moon. Since studio head Louis B. Mayer was no bibliophile, Marion had little trouble convincing him that she had based *Min and Bill* on Moon's novel, *Dark Star*. That, of course, was a bald-faced lie, but Mayer never caught on to the scam, and the desperately ill Ms. Moon was able to finance treatment in a T.B. sanitarium when MGM paid for the rights to "her" story.

A former *San Francisco Examiner* reporter and one of the few women correspondents to cover battles in World War I, this unsung heroine also hosted weekly "cat sessions" for women in the film industry, defied her male bosses to help found the Screen Writers Guild, and annoyed the heck out of Mayer by using her twin Oscars (for *The Big House* and *The Champ*) as doorstops. "You never did take the business serious enough," he grumbled when he noticed the lowly role to which she relegated those coveted film industry trophies. But the cigar-chomping mogul was dead wrong—Marion just happened to have a more inclusive "business" plan in mind.

> *"I hope my story shows one thing—how many women gave me real aid when I stood at the crossroads."*
>
> —MF

BOOTSTRAPPING BABE

The founder of her own independent production company, director Ida Lupino never went to film school. She learned her craft as a bored Warner Brothers actress during the 1940s. "I paid attention," she later recalled. "I didn't like to stand around wasting time."

Lupino: One self-directed dame

THE PETERED-OUT PRINCIPLE

Lucy Fisher didn't distinguish herself during her stint as a United Artists manuscript reader in the 1970s—or, perhaps, she did. "This is really terrible, and it's too boring even to tell you why," was the comment the weary script-winnower typically gave to her boss. Fisher wound up as executive vice-president of Warner Brothers.

Hellish Louella

The grande dame of Hollywood dish in the 1930s and '40s, Louella Parsons essentially invented the movie gossip column, and the savage pen she wielded could make or break a star's career. Born in 1881, Parsons got a toehold in the prose biz as a *Chicago Tribune* reporter. The job barely paid the rent, however, and the future empress of innuendo moonlighted as a movie scenario writer. In 1914, she launched one of the first U.S. movie columns for the *Chicago Record-Herald*, and eventually wound up as a protégé of publishing magnate (and big movie star fan) William Randolph Hearst.

Hearst brought Parsons to Hollywood, and from 1926 through 1964 she cranked out the bean-spilling column that was eventually syndicated in hundreds of publications. A titillating mélange of tidbits about actors' private lives and information about their public careers, Parsons' few-holds-barred reports set the standard for a genre that has seldom been varied from since. Writing under the informal byline "Tell It To Louella," she courted informants, cultivated useful friends (Clark Gable, Mary Pickford, Rita Hayworth), and built a vast network of sources. One of which, incidentally, happened to be her husband, Dr. Harry Watson Martin, head of the Twentieth Century-Fox medical department. Thanks to the good doc, Parsons had a private line to medical testing laboratories, and often knew the results of a star's rabbit test before the mama-to-be had even received the news.

Factual errors were frequent, and Parsons was known for her unintentional howlers. "Ingrid, Ingrid, whatever got into you?" she scolded when wholesome Ingrid Bergman became pregnant out of wedlock. But neither her hilarious boo-boos nor the emergence of rival tell-tale Hedda Hopper in the late 1930s made Parsons any less loved by her

The callous columnist at work

readership—or any more so by the stars who feared her. As no less a powermeister than Samuel Goldwyn once quipped: "Louella Parsons is stronger than Samson. He needed two columns to bring the house down. Louella can do it with one."

"Hollywood is and has been my life."
—LP

WHAT'S WRONG WITH THIS PICTURE?

Studying his part in *The Big Sleep* in 1946, Humphrey Bogart found some of the dialogue too tepid for his taste. Since writers Leigh Brackett (a woman) and William Faulkner (a man) had teamed up on the script, Bogie was startled to learn that it wasn't the gal who gave him the sissy lines. Unlike HB, however, *Big Sleep* director Howard Hawks at least made an effort not to stereotype Brackett (whom he went on to hire again and again) on the basis of her sex. In fact, Hawks bestowed upon the macha scribe—whose final Hollywood script would be *The Empire Strikes Back* in 1980—the highest "praise" in his pre-feminist book: "She wrote like a man."

Horrible Hedda

*I*f Louella Parsons was known as a perfect bitch—well, Hedda Hopper was a bitch on wheels. Not to mention a self-satisfied one: as she herself snickered, her lavish Beverly Hills home really ought to be called "The House That Fear Built."

Born Elda Furry in 1885, the budding battle-ax once harbored movie star ambitions herself. Known in Hollywood as the "Queen of the Quickies" in the late 1920s, she appeared in supporting roles in scores of movies, but fame and fortune eluded her. In fact, the second-string actress—who upgraded her name on a numerologist's advice—also sold real estate and modeled for a mail-order catalogue in order to make ends meet. Finally, a career consultant suggested that she launch a radio gossip show—and voilà! a star (of sorts, anyway) was born.

Using her broadcasting success as a springboard, Hopper made her debut as a gossip columnist in 1938. At first, her efforts attracted little notice. But "the minute I started to trot out the juicy stuff," she noted, "my phone began to ring." The following year, she scooped Parsons on the divorce of President Roosevelt's son, thereby launching a life-long feud with her competitor, and establishing herself as a contender. Within a few years, her column would be syndicated in eighty-five metropolitan and 3,000 small-town dailies—and her reputation as a vindictive, megalomaniac shrew would outstrip that of Parsons.

Hopper was famous, of course, for her vendettas against certain celebrities: Elsa Maxwell, Constance Bennett, and Charlie Chaplin, to name only a few, frequently found themselves on the biting end of that venemous pen. So did Michael Wilding, Elizabeth Taylor's second husband, whom Hopper once insinuated was gay. "You rattled, dried-up, frustrated old c***," raged one of Wilding's more infuriated friends, who chewed out the columnist by telephone. (Wilding later sued for libel, and won.) But as far as Hopper was

The first lady of poison pen lettres

concerned, it seems, the howls of her victims were merely a hazard of her highly lucrative occupation. After all, she once wrote, "Nobody is interested in sweetness and light."

"You can't fool an old bag like me."
—HH

THE SCOOP ON THE SNOOPS

"Hedda Hopper and Louella Parsons. They were bitches!"
—**Elizabeth Taylor**

"They were a demented pair, and Hollywood was even more demented for allowing them so much power over people's careers and lives."
—**Gale Sondergaard**

"Hedda and Louella would have been jokes except for their power."
—**Jim Backus**, *Gilligan's Island* **actor**

"She's a quaint old udder, isn't she?"
—**John Barrymore, Sr., of Parsons**

"Take one black widow spider, cross it with a scorpion; wean their poisonous offspring on a mixture of prussic acid and treacle, and you'll get the honeyed sting of Hedda Hopper."
—**Author David Zec, of Hopper**

"When we cursed them collectively, we referred to them as Lulu Poppers."
—**Lili Palmer**

One Helluva Hostess

"I'm fat, dingy and oversized, but I don't care," shrugged Elsa Maxwell, the accomplished actress (and author and composer and, most famously, professional party-thrower) whose antics astonished and amused Hollywood in the late '30s and early '40s. At five feet and 196 pounds, Maxwell was certainly more massive than your standard Tinseltown beauty. Yet her myriad well-placed friends and admirers included Aristotle Onassis, at least two Princes of Monaco (one of whom hired her to popularize the casinos of Monte Carlo in the 1920s), and George Bernard Shaw (who simply considered her "the eighth wonder of the world").

Though Maxwell may well have entered the world with a spoon in her mouth, it certainly wasn't the silver kind. Born in an Iowa opera box in 1883 (Mama Maxwell took in a performance of *Mignon* while giving birth), she was a child prodigy who could play anything by ear "on any instrument that came within my reach." But while Mom and Pop were big on culture, they were short on cash, and so the girl who might have been Mozart went to work as a teen, earning her keep as a movie theater pianist and a member of a traveling Shakespeare troupe. She went on to compose some eighty songs (and one major symphony), accompany opera greats Enrico Caruso and Nellie Melba, and perform vaudeville acts around the globe.

But it was her *other* world-class talent, a serious gift for having fun, that endeared Maxwell to all she encountered—which seems to have included just about everyone who was anyone in the Western hemisphere during World Wars I and II. To this day, no one knows quite how she carved out her career as a hostess to the movers and shakers she met. ("Miss Maxwell was neither beautiful nor wealthy nor socially prominent," the *New York Times* observed upon her death in 1963, "and it was a great mystery how she got to the position of social prominence she reached and held for more than forty years.") But by the mid-1930s, the once-impoverished Iowan was the woman the rich and the royal depended on to host a truly distinctive do.

"Anything, so long as it's different," proclaimed Maxwell, whose soirée-enhancing stunts included setting a bunch of live seals loose in a ballroom, forcing debutantes to milk cows for a charity auction, staging murder mysteries for guests to solve, and inventing (so she claimed) the scavenger hunt. And certainly the celebrated hostess did not disappoint in Hollywood, where she landed in 1938, and promptly proceeded to distribute live ducklings, bedecked in blue and white ribbons, as favors at a bash for her pal the Duchess of Westminster.

Her short-lived film career, on the other hand, was not quite as noteworthy (Maxwell essentially played—or publicized—herself in pictures with titles like *Elsa Maxwell's Hotel for Women* [1939] and *Elsa Maxwell's Public Deb Number One* [1940]). But the madcap multi-careerist (who subsequently achieved more significant success as, among other things, a radio actress, a T.V. personality, and a syndicated gossip columnist) simply shrugged when critics called her a beached "baby whale," an "Eskimo igloo," or "the fattest frump alive." "How about the late Eleanor Roosevelt and Wanda Landowska, or even the Duchess of Windsor?" Maxwell would later write. "None of these ladies became what they are because they were lovely to look at, and none of them let plainness stand in their way. Indeed, they probably never gave the matter a thought; they were too busy moving ahead."

"Moving ahead" might well have been Maxwell's personal motto—except for the fact that she lived by an even better one: "Down with boredom!"

"I've always been laughed at, but I've never been ignored."
—EM

THE WRATH OF CANNES

In 1972, screenwriter Eleanor Perry traveled all the way to the Cannes Film Festival to read sexist moviemakers the riot act. Armed with red paint and the slogan "women are people, not dirty jokes," the wrathful writer and her cohorts managed to stir up quite a ruckus. "You wouldn't know women were part of the human race from most of the films," she later said. One of Perry's better-known movies, incidentally, is *Diary of a Mad Housewife.*

"If a man wants to get it right, he's looked up to and respected. If a woman wants to get it right, she's difficult and impossible. If he acts, produces, and directs, he's called multi-talented. If she does the same thing, she's called vain and egotistical."
—**Barbra Streisand, the famously difficult, impossible, vain, and egotistical actress/producer/director**

"AND WHAT WAS *YOUR* COLLEGE MAJOR, MISS BASINGER?"

Perhaps you run with a glitzier crowd than the rest of us. Perhaps you once found yourself standing next to Sharon Stone, say, in the 12-items-or-less check-out lane—and wound up so severely tongue-tied that you'd have been in serious nutritional trouble if you were an anteater instead of you. Or perhaps your name is Bret Saxon or Steve Stein, your avocation is celebrity schmoozing, and you're so obsessed with the topic of *How to Meet and Hang Out with the Stars* that you've actually co-authored a book by that name.

Whatever your reason for expending precious gray matter (or, more to the point, precious green material) on the subject of chatting up celebrities, *How to Meet and Hang Out with the Stars* offers many thought-provoking suggestions. Following are some beauts that Saxon and Stein suggest you broach the next time you're face to face with one of our reigning vamps, vixens, or sirens:

Geena Davis:	"Her marriage"
Cher:	"Her current hit infomercials"
Brett Butler:	"Her cool first name"
Julia Roberts:	"Her early ambition to become a veterinarian"
Demi Moore:	"Her husband"
Shannen Doherty:	"Her early roles"
Jodie Foster:	"Her ability to read at the age of three"
Kim Basinger:	"Her college life at Southern Methodist University"
Goldie Hawn:	"Her 'husband' (they're not actually married)"

Of course, if "Tell me about your 'husband,' Miss Hawn," fails to spring the conversational floodgates, you *could* bring up the weather, the NBA playoffs, the lead story in today's newspaper—or how very, very bizarrely human beings can sometimes behave.

Bibliography

BOOKS

Amende, Coral. *Hollywood Confidential*. New York: Penguin, 1997.

Anger, Kenneth. *Hollywood Babylon*. New York: Dell, 1975.

_____. *Hollywood Babylon II*. New York: Penguin, 1984.

Balazs, André, ed. *The Chateau Marmont's Hollywood Handbook*. New York: Universe Publishing, 1996.

Ballenger, Seale. *Hell's Belles*. Berkeley, CA: Conari Press, 1997.

Bernikow, Louise. *The American Women's Almanac*. New York: Berkley Books, 1997.

Boller, Paul F., and Ronald L. Davis. *Hollywood Anecdotes*. New York: William Morrow, 1987.

Case, Christopher. *The Ultimate Movie Thesaurus*. New York: Henry Holt, 1996.

Cawthorne, Nigel. *Sex Lives of The Hollywood Goddesses*. London: PRION, 1997.

_____. *Sex Lives of The Hollywood Idols*. London: PRION, 1997.

Dietrich, Marlene. *Marlene Dietrich's ABC.* New York: Frederick Ungar, 1984.

Forbes, Malcolm. *Women Who Made A Difference*. New York: Simon and Schuster, 1990.

Hadleigh, Boze. *Hollywood Babble On*. New York: Berkley Publishing, 1994.

_____. *Hollywood Lesbians*. New York: Barricade Books, 1994.

Hine, Denise Clark, ed. *Black Women In America: An Historical Encyclopedia*. Bloomington, IN: Indiana University Press, 1993.

Hofstede, David. *First Appearances*. Las Vegas, NV: Zanne-3 Publishing, 1996.

Katz, Ephraim. *The Film Encyclopedia*. New York: HarperCollins, 1994.

Leider, Emily Wortis. *Becoming Mae West*. New York: Farrar, Straus and Giroux, 1997.

Levin, Eric, ed. *The Most Intriguing People of the Century*. New York: People Weekly Books, 1997.

Macdonald, Anne L. *Feminine Ingenuity*. New York: Ballantine Books, 1992.

Madsen, Axel. *Forbidden Lovers*. Seacaucus, NJ: Carol Publishing, 1996.

Maggio, Rosalie. *The Beacon Book of Quotations by Women*. Boston: Beacon Press, 1992.

Martin, Mart. *Did She Or Didn't She? Behind the Bedroom Doors of 201 Famous Women*. New York: Citadel Press, 1996.

Maxwell, Elsa. *The Celebrity Circus*. New York: Appleton-Century, 1963.

Richards, Dell. *Lesbian Lists*. Boston: Alyson Publications, 1990.

Saxon, Bret, and Steve Stein. *How to Meet and Hang Out With the Stars*. New York: Citadel Press, 1990.

Seger, Linda. *When Women Call the Shots*. New York: Henry Holt, 1996.

Sicherman, Barbara, and Carol Hurd Green, eds. *Notable American Women: The Modern Period*. Cambridge, MA: Radcliffe College, 1980.

Uglow, Jennifer S. *The Continuum Dictionary of Women's Biography*. New York: Continuum, 1989.

Weintraub, Joseph, ed. *The Wit and Wisdom of Mae West*. New York: G. P. Putnam, 1967.

Wiley, Mason, and Damien Bona. *Inside Oscar*. New York: Ballantine Books, 1996.

Zaslow, Jeffrey. *Talk of Fame*. New York: Cader Books, 1997.

Zophy, Angela Howard, and Frances M. Kavenik, eds. *Handbook of American Women's History*. New York: Garland Reference Library of the Humanities, 1990.

PERIODICALS

Arnold, Chuck. "Chatter" column, *People*, January 12, 1998.

Beauchamp, Cari. "Even for Talkies, They Worked Silently." *The New York Times*, June 22, 1997.

Bernstein, Jill. "Ida Lupino." *Premiere*, Women in Hollywood Special Issue, 1998.

Carpenter, Sue. "The Nerve of Her." *Jane*, March 1998.

DiLucchio, Patrizia. "All That and Brains Too." *People*, April 7, 1997.

Garchik, Leah. "Personals" column, *San Francisco Chronicle*, March 20, 1998.

Gliatto, Tom. "Darling." *People*, February 9, 1998.

Lauderdale, Beverly. "The Lady Lived The Blues." *Biography*, February 1998.

Magnuson, Ann. "Ugly Like Me." *Allure*, January 1998.

O'Neal, P. J. "Starwatch" column, *Marie Claire*, January 1998.

Scott, Walter. "Personality Parade" column, *Parade*, February 15, 1998.

Sischy, Ingrid. "Madonna and Child." *Vanity Fair*, March 1998.

Sorensen, Holly, ed. "In a League of Their Own." *Premiere*, Women in Hollywood Special Issue, 1993._____. "Reelin' In the Years." *Ibid*. Young, Tracy. "Beauty and the Beat." *Allure*, March 1998.

Index

Wild Women Association

In 1992, with the publication of *Wild Women* by Autumn Stephens, Conari Press founded the Wild Women Association. Today there are over 3,000 card-carrying Wild Women in cities throughout the world—and some even meet regularly with their untamed and uproarious sisters specifically to encourage unbridled behavior. The Association's primary purpose is to rediscover and rewrite our wild predecessors back into history. If there is a wild woman in your family, please help by sending us information for possible inclusion in subsequent volumes of the "Wild and Ever-So-Uppity Women" series.

To become a member and to receive the Wild Women Association Newsletter, please mail this page to:

The Wild Women Association
2550 Ninth Street, Suite 101
Berkeley, CA 94710-2551

Let's rewrite history with women in it!

Wild Women in the Kitchen
101 Rambunctious Recipes & 99 Tasty Tales
by The Wild Women Association

Wild Words from Wild Women
An Unbridled Collection of Candid Observations
& Extremely Opinionated Bon Mots
by Autumn Stephens

Conari Press, established in 1987, publishes books on topics
ranging from spirituality and women's history to sexuality and
personal growth. Our main goal is to publish quality books
that will make a difference in people's lives—both
how we feel about ourselves and how
we relate to one another.

Our readers are our most important resource, and
we value your input, suggestions, and ideas. We'd love to hear
from you—after all, we are publishing books for you!

For a complete catalog or to be added to our mailing list,
please contact:

CONARI PRESS
2550 Ninth Street, Suite 101
Berkeley, California 94710-2551

Tel: 800-685-9595   Fax: 510-649-7190
E-mail: Conaripub@aol.com